S0-DHW-861

Andy liu

andyxliu@gmail.com

New York, NY

may 2007

History, Rhetoric, and Proof

THE MENAHEM STERN JERUSALEM LECTURES

sponsored by the Historical Society of Israel
and published for Brandeis University Press by
University Press of New England

HISTORY, RHETORIC, and PROOF

Carlo Ginzburg

THE MENAHEM STERN JERUSALEM LECTURES

 Brandeis
University
Press

 Historical
Society of
Israel

PUBLISHED BY UNIVERSITY PRESS OF NEW ENGLAND

Hanover and London

Brandeis University Press/Historical Society of Israel

Published by University Press of New England, Hanover, NH 03755

© 1999 by Historical Society of Israel

All rights reserved

Printed in the United States of America   5 4 3 2 1

CIP data appear at the end of the book

to Italo Calvino and Arnaldo Momigliano

Contents

Foreword

Yosef Kaplan

Four years have already passed since that bitter day when Menahem Stern was taken from us—more than four years since we were shocked to hear the dreadful news of the murder of our beloved teacher and dear friend on his way to the National Library, a path he used to take every day. Time has not healed this wound. It has not closed. The passing years only heighten the feeling we all have of being orphaned, and the sense that no one can fill the void he left.

It was a comfort for us to take shelter beneath his roof and to be able to count on his enormous erudition, upon which we constantly drew and from which we took endless assistance. We miss his sound advice, which always combined rich life experience, sober intelligence, a generous heart, and love of his fellow man. We miss that glowing and noble figure, sitting in the Jewish Studies Reading Room or in the Periodical Room of the National Library, with towering stacks of books and journals before him. Engraved in our memory is the picture of him walking to the corner of the Classics Library carrying a bundle of proofs of *Zion*, the Hebrew quarterly for research in Jewish history published by the Historical Society of Israel, of which he was an editor for many years, for a very rigorous person was hidden beneath his good nature and affability. This rigor was expressed first of all in his research in the sources of Jewish history during the Second Temple period and the history of the Hellenistic and Roman world. Let me mention two of his works here: *The Documents on the History of the Hasmonean Revolt*, and especially the three volumes of his monumental *Greek and Latin Authors on Jews and Judaism*.

Stern was also outstanding in his profound and detailed articles, where he succeeded, with unique virtuosity, in evoking a broad

Address inaugurating the Jerusalem Lectures in History in Memory of Menahem Stern, 7 December 1993.

and full historical picture through detailed discussion. These articles were meant to be the preparation for a comprehensive book about the Second Temple period. He had been immersed in the writing of that book during the last years of his life, but was unable to complete it because of the deadly hand that struck him down. He bequeathed us a huge scholarly achievement to serve as a model and as an example for future generations, for every one of its parts and details reflects uncompromising scholarly rigor and faithfulness to the methods and the most stringent demands of the historical discipline. Not only did Stern determine a high level of research in one of the central fields of Jewish history, but he also created scholarly standards that are an example for every Jewish historian, whatever his field may be.

The Historical Society of Israel decided to establish a special lecture series in memory of Menahem Stern. Every year a historian of the first rank is invited to give a series of three lectures. The guest must be one of the major historians of our time, by virtue of his unique contribution to historical research. The lectures are to be on historical, historiographical, or comparative subjects, or on monographic topics with broad consequences for the discipline of history.

It is a great honour for the Historical Society of Israel and for the Israeli community of historians that the first distinguished scholar to present the Stern Lectures is Professor Carlo Ginzburg, of the University of California, Los Angeles, one of the most original and prolific historians of our generation.

He received his training as a historian at the Scuola Normale Superiore of Pisa, where he studied with, among others, Delio Cantimori, one of his esteemed teachers. Following in Cantimori's footsteps, Ginzburg has also devoted a considerable part of his work to the study of Italian religious radicals of the sixteenth century, though he has done this in independent fashion, both in his choice of subjects and in his methodology. For independence and intellectual openness are the central characteristics of Ginzburg's historiographical work. The main focus of his research has been Italy of the sixteenth and seventeenth centuries, and the subjects of his research may be placed in a number of central categories: the study of religious radicals, investigations of witchcraft and popular culture, research on iconography, and studies in historiography.

His book *Il Nicodemismo* on the Nicodemites is a masterpiece in intellectual history and biography, a product of true detective work in ferreting out iconographical and historical sources. In his fine book *The Enigma of Piero*, about three major works by the fifteenth-century artist Piero della Francesca, Ginzburg analyzed the iconography and the patrons of these works. However, any brief description of Ginzburg's work does an injustice to an oeuvre distinguished by true uniqueness. In all of his works, Ginzburg demonstrates broad and profound knowledge of various periods and cultures, and it is difficult to find any area of human life which has not aroused his insatiable intellectual curiosity: philology, the study of religion, philosophy, art, anthropology, folklore, psychoanalysis. However, even though he makes use of various disciplines and even though his work is virtually a paean in praise of the interdisciplinary approach, Ginzburg remains faithful to the *métier de l'historien.*

As a young man he wanted to be a novelist. Later he thought of becoming a painter, until his teachers persuaded him to be a historian. The benefit belongs entirely to modern historiography, which has been privileged to enjoy the contribution of one of the most talented and innovative scholars of the past. However, art has not lost out: all of his books are not only masterpieces with respect to their content, but they can also be read as fascinating novels, for they are picturesque and stirring pictures painted by an artist-historian.

In *I Benandanti*, known in its English translation as *The Night Battles*, in *Il formaggio e i vermi (The Cheese and the Worms)* and in his more recent *Storia Notturna*, known in its English translation as *Ecstasies* (a fascinating journey through many centuries of human history, in which the author has penetrated to the deep levels of both European and Asian culture), he has opened up new vistas upon European popular culture in the late Middle Ages and the early modern period. Not only has he called our attention to the ways in which the learned culture tried to suppress and dominate popular culture, but with his virtuosity he has also pointed out the vitality of popular culture and the means by which it retained its independence and even, in its own way, influenced elite and establishment culture. To that end Ginzburg has mobilized the best of the Inquisitors, whom he turned into anthropologists despite themselves, and by means of their investigations he has penetrated to the depths of the world of peasants and common people, showing how complex and vital was their culture.

Not only has he laid bare the spiritual world of the miller Menocchio, having traced the creative misreadings of that fascinating figure, but he has also permitted us to understand that as long as we are unable to reconstruct the world of Marcato "and so many others like him who lived and died without leaving a trace," our knowledge of the past will lack a vital component, the search for which and the revelation of its place in human history are an important goal of historical science.

Dear Carlo Ginzburg, we thank you for coming and sharing your learning with us. Thank you for the many hours of true intellectual pleasure and stimulation that you have given to all those who have eagerly read your works. We are certain that you shall continue, as is fitting for a historian of the *benandanti* like yourself, to fight in spirit for the intellectual fertility of the historical discipline.

And now: "Aristotle and History—Once more." Carlo Ginzburg—Once more.

ACKNOWLEDGMENTS

I have an unforgettable memory of my days in Jerusalem. I should like to thank the families of Menahem Stern and of Zvi Yekutiel for the honor of inviting me, and Yosef Kaplan for his warm hospitality and his patience. The preparation of this small volume has ended up being more difficult than anticipated. The revisions begun at the Getty Center in Santa Monica in 1995 were only concluded in Berlin at the Wissenschaftskolleg in 1997. I am grateful to both institutions for their hospitality and support. Many people came to my assistance with their suggestions and criticisms. I should like to thank Pier Cesare Bori, Maria Luisa Catoni, Mordechai Feingold, and Alberto Gajano (for the introduction); Gianna Pomata and, especially, Julia Annas (for the first chapter); Matthew S. Kempshall (for the second); Gisela Bock, Mordechai Feingold, and John Elliott (for the third); Saul Friedländer, Paul Holdengräber, and Franco Moretti (for the fourth). The errors that remain, naturally, are my own.

The first three chapters are versions of lectures originally presented in Jerusalem, which have appeared, respectively, in Italian in *Quaderni storici* 85, no. 29 (April 1994); in French as an introduction to L. Valla, *La donation de Constantin* (Paris, 1993); in Greek in *Ta Istorika-Historica* 12, no. 22 (June 1995). All the texts have been revised and updated for this publication. The introduction and the fourth lecture appear here for the first time.

I am extremely grateful to John and Anne Tedeschi for the skill and friendship with which, once again, they came to my assistance, translating the introduction and revising the text and notes.

Bologna   C.G.
August 1998

History, Rhetoric, and Proof

Introduction

I

History, rhetoric, proof: in this sequence, the least obvious term today is the last. The widely accepted contiguity between history and rhetoric has pushed aside the one between history and proof. The idea that historians should or can prove anything seems an antiquated idea to many, if not downright ridiculous. But even people who feel qualms over the dominant intellectual climate almost always consider it inevitable that rhetoric and proof should exclude one another.[1] Instead, I want to demonstrate that (a) in the past, proof was considered an integral part of rhetoric, and (b) this once obvious fact, now forgotten, implies an image of the working methods of historians, including our contemporaries, that is much more realistic and complex than the one fashionable today.

II

The skeptical theses based on the reduction of historiography to its narrative or rhetorical dimension have been in circulation for a few decades, even if their roots, as we shall see, are more ancient. In general, the theoreticians of historiography who propose them care little for the concrete work of historians. But even historians, aside from some token homage to a "linguistic turn" or "rhetorical turn" currently in vogue, are scarcely inclined to reflect on the theoretical implications of their own profession. Rarely has the chasm between methodological reflection and actual historiographical practice been as pronounced as in the last few decades. It seems that the only way to overcome it is to take the challenge of the skeptics seriously and attempt to articulate the point of view of those who work in contact with documents, in the broadest sense of the term. My solution transfers to the actuality of research the tensions between narration and documentation. It does not propose a rapprochement between theoreticians and historians, and probably will displease them both.

These subjects would seem at first to concern only a small circle of adepts actually involved in these labors: historians, philosophers, students of the methodology of history. But this is a deceptive notion. As we shall see, the discussion on history, rhetoric, and proof touches on a question that concerns us all: the coexistence and clash between cultures. To many of us it seems right that we should accept the existence of customs and values different from ours; to accept them always and in every form seems intolerable to some, including to me. We can adopt a pragmatic posture, deciding case by case: the Islamic veil and infibulation are quite different things. But even the Islamic veil, as we saw in France a few years ago (and as we see today in Algeria, with infinitely more tragic consequences) raises questions of principle that cannot be avoided.[2] Do we have the right to impose our laws, our customs, and our values on people from other cultures?

For a few centuries, European nations took such a right for granted in the midst of their colonial expansion, even if the justification for it varied: from right and duty, linked to a civilization that deemed itself superior, to the right of the more powerful, to, usually, a combination of those two notions. Today, in an age in which coexistence, often an uneasy one, between different cultures has shifted to the metropolis, one hears from all sides that the moral and cognitive principles of the various cultures are not comparable. This attitude, which in theory should result in unlimited tolerance, paradoxically originates from premises similar to those that inspire the principle equating right with might. We could speak of skeptical relativism in two versions, one meek (in intentions, even if not always in consequences) and the other ferocious. These positions, which are politically so distant, if not actually opposed, have a common intellectual origin: an idea of rhetoric that is not only foreign, but actually opposed, to proof.[3] It is an idea that goes back to Nietzsche. Its genesis, both distant and near, throws unexpected light on contemporary discussions concerning relations between dissimilar cultures.

III

Nietzsche frequently spoke with admiration about Thucydides; on one occasion he alluded to the "terrible" dialogue between Athenians and Melians.[4] The setting for the dialogue is well known: in the course of the almost three-decade-long Peloponnesian War fought between Sparta and Athens, and their respective allies, the inhabitants of the island of Melos, a colony of Sparta, had tried at first to remain neutral; later, in the face of overbearing demands by the Athenians, they rebelled. The Athenians responded with a bloody repression in 416, killing the men of Melos, and reducing the women and children to slavery.[5] Politically and militarily this was an event of slight significance, but Thucydides decided to give it great prominence: he precedes his brief account of the punishment meted out to the rebels of Melos with a long dialogue, which occupies chapters 85 through 113 in the fifth book of his work. To the Melians who invoke arguments connected to the cause of justice, the Athenians oppose, implacably, the reasons of power: "Since you know as well as we do that, when these matters are discussed by practical people, the standard of justice depends on the equality of power to compel and that in fact the strong do what they have the power to do and the weak accept what they have to accept" (5.89).

The Melians assert that they trust in the protection of the gods whom they have always honored, and of the Spartans, their allies. No one will protect them, the Athenians reply. Everyone, men and gods, must submit to the natural necessity that impels whoever has power to exercise it, everywhere and in whatever circumstance. Even the Athenians accept this necessity: "This is not a law that we made ourselves, nor were we the first to act upon it when it was made. We found it already in existence, and we shall leave it to exist forever among those who come after us" (5.105). And so forth.

Thucydides, as Dionysius of Halicarnassus observed three centuries later, was an exile in Thrace: he could not have had direct or even indirect evidence of the dialogue between the Athenians and the Melians. In the opinion of Dionysius this did not explain its improbability. It was improbable, he argued, because the Athenians could never have dealt so brutally with other Greeks without even mentioning justice. Thucydides was thereby violating the very criteria he had himself adopted to justify the inclusion of discourse in his work (1.22). Dionysius supposes that Thucydides was writing moved by anger towards the city that had exiled him. Another observation, to which Dionysius returns twice, enters, instead, into the heart of the structure of the dialogue: while the first sallies refer to the speech of others, what follows takes a dramatic form.[6]

Let's look then at how the dialogue begins. The Athenians declare that the Melians have requested that the meeting not be held before the assembly: "no doubt in case the mass of the people should hear once and for all and without interruption an argument from us which is both persuasive and incontrovertible, and should so be led astray" (5.85).

It has been supposed that these words describe the way the colloquy really occurred, an interpretation that, in my opinion, should be rejected.[7] It is more reasonable to suppose that they offer a key for reading what will follow. The "uninterrupted discourse" based on argumentation that the Melians denounce as "persuasive," "incontrovertible"—a technical term—is the discourse of rhetoric, intended to seek out popular consensus. Opposed to it is the dialogue behind closed doors, in which it will be possible to discuss "without fine talk" (5.89), without deceit or worries about consensus, matters that normally should be hidden from the majority.[8]

Nietzsche, who admired Thucydides as a master of realism free of moralizing scruples, probably took it for granted that he agreed with the Athenians.[9] Someone, taking a cue from Nietzsche, has maintained that Thucydides could not have failed to recognize the superiority of the Athenian arguments, seeing that the course of events had vindicated them.[10] This conclusion is debatable for two reasons. On the one hand, it has not been demonstrated that Thucydides equated right with success. On the other, in the long run, success, as we know, did not at all favor the Athenians. This brings up the long-contested question of the date of Thucydides' work. The threatening allusion made by the Melians to the possibility that the Athenians would be defeated in their turn (5.90) appears to situate the composition of the dialogue, as well as perhaps most of the work, after 404: Thucydides would have been trying to demonstrate through an exemplary case the imperialistic arrogance that had dragged Athens to ruin.[11] Thucydides, a confirmed critic of

Athenian democracy, probably even agreed with the polemic against rhetoric as an art intended to seduce "the majority" with attractive and fallacious arguments, which the Athenians attributed to the oligarchic and philo-Spartan Melians at the beginning of the dialogue.[12]

against
rhet

IV

The arguments the Athenians adopted in their discussion with the Melians recall closely, as scholars have often mentioned, those of Callicles, one of the interlocutors of the *Gorgias*, which Plato wrote shortly after 387. This resemblance has generally been traced to an extratextual fact, namely Callicles' ideas, which, however, have come down to us only through the *Gorgias*.[13] It would be more prudent if we limited ourselves to a comparison between the two texts, the exchanges between the Athenians and the Melians, and the Platonic dialogue. We shall see that such an exercise will take us back to Nietzsche.

Just a short way into the work, Socrates pleads with the rhetorician Gorgias to continue "the discussion in the way we are having it right now, alternatively asking questions and answering them, and to put aside for another time this long style of speechmaking," in which another interlocutor, Polus, had expressed himself. Here too, as in Thucydides, the long speeches of the rhetoricians must give way to concise discourse, based, on the one hand, on the alternation of questions and answers, and, on the other, on confutation.[14] After observing that to refute an idea does not signify launching a personal attack against the person who proposed it, Socrates declares that he is one who prefers to be refuted rather than to refute (458a): an elegant anticipation of the provocative thesis proposed a little later, which states that it is better to suffer injustice than to commit it.[15] Gorgias is invited to accept these provisions; otherwise, says Socrates, it would be better to break off the discussion at once. Analogously, before undertaking his discussion with Polus, Socrates warns: "take your turn in asking and being asked questions the way Gorgias and I did, and subject me and yourself to refutation" (462a).

In the course of the dialogue Socrates denounces rhetoric as a "deceiving" art (465b), comparable to other forms of "adulation," such as sophistry, cosmesis, and cuisine (463b). They are the distorted image of justice, of legislation, of gymnastics, and of medicine: the first two, arts linked to the soul (or rather to politics); the last two, arts linked to the body. On the basis of this classification, the structure of the *Gorgias* appears wholly coherent.[16] The arts discussed along the way—rhetoric, justice, politics—belong to a single sphere, that of the soul: the first, because it is a distortion of the second; the third, because it is a more general art including both (together with legislation and its distorted version, sophistry).

Socrates asserts that it is better to suffer injustice than to commit it, and Polus ends up agreeing with him. Callicles interrupts indignantly, contrasting nature and law and accusing Socrates in his arguments of slipping unduly from one to the other: "for by nature all that is more evil is also more shameful, such as suffering the unjust, whereas doing it by law is more shameful." To tolerate wrongs is fitting not for men but for slaves. Legislators, who are the weakest and the most numerous, make laws thinking of their self-interest. Since they are inferior, they are happy enough to be equals. This sarcastic quip demonstrates that Callicles' ideas, despite his efforts to ingratiate himself at all costs with the Athenian people (as Socrates reproaches him), are far from being democratic:[17] "nature itself reveals that it's a just thing for the better man and the more capable man to have a greater share than the inferior man and the less capable man" (483c).

The introduction of the notion of justice in the realm of nature announces reasoning similar to the Athenians' in their dialogue with the Melians. This resemblance becomes even closer, as we have noted, where Callicles overcomes the traditional opposition between *physis* and *nomos*, "nature" and "law" (or "convention") to assert that the dominion of the strong over the weak is a law (5.105), as the Athenians had argued in their confrontation with the Melians: "I believe that these men do these things in accordance with the nature of what's just—yes, by Zeus, in accordance with the law of nature, and presumably not with the one we institute" (483e).[18]

Did Plato know the work of Thucydides? There has been much discussion over this hypothesis, usually concluding negatively.[19] According to a number of interpreters, even the convergence just mentioned would demonstrate only that both Thucydides and Plato were reacting to ideas then current in Athens in circles influenced by the sophists.[20] But the statement by Callicles, if reinserted in context, suggests a direct relationship with Thucydides' text:

Nature itself reveals that it's a just thing for the better man and the more capable man to have a greater share than the inferior man and the less capable man. Nature shows that this is so in many places; both among the other animals and in whole cities and races of men, it shows that this is what justice has been decided to be: that the superior rule the inferior and have a greater share than they. For what sort of justice did Xerxes go by when he campaigned against Greece, or his father when he campaigned against Scythia? Countless other such examples could be mentioned. (483d–e)

Is this intentionally paradoxical discourse meant to suggest that even the punishment of Melos, which by now had become part of anti-Athenian propaganda, should be included among these countless cases?[21] This hypothesis is strengthened by the already quoted words, which follow immediately, on "the law of nature" as the law of the strongest: "in accordance with the law of nature, and presumably not with the one we institute." Once again, those terms echo Thucydides: "This is not a law that we made ourselves, nor were we the first to act upon it when it was made. We found it already in existence, and we shall leave it to exist forever among those who come after us" (5.105).

The expression "to enact a law" is quite banal. But far from banal at that time was the idea of using the term "law" in regard to nature: to the point that both the Athenians and Callicles felt the need to specify "laws yes, but not enacted by us." The *Gorgias* was written a few years after the conclusion of the Peloponnesian War. Along with Thucydides, and inspired by even more explicitly antidemocratic sentiments, Plato attempted to comprehend how the tragedy had occurred.[22] At the end of a sharp attack against Athenian democracy, turning to Callicles, Socrates exclaims: "You've made me deliver a really popular harangue" (519d). These words echoed, in a tone of jesting challenge, Callicles' earlier reproach that he was "acting like a true crowd pleaser" (482c).[23] But the playful retort has a serious basis: it is philosophers and not rhetoricians who know what politics means. "I believe that I'm one of a few Athenians," Socrates exclaimed provocatively, "—not to say I'm the only one, but the only one among our contemporaries—to take up the true political craft and practice the true politics" (521d). Plato laid the blame for the defeat of Athens on its politicians and on Pericles in particular. The attack against rhetoric launched in the *Gorgias* originated in this climate, and with a bitter antidemocratic connotation.

V

We can imagine the emotions experienced by the young philologist Nietzsche when he read the *Gorgias* for the first time.[24] Domination of the strong over the weak dictated by a law of nature to which individuals, peoples, and states are subject; morality and law as projections of the interests of the weakling majority; submission to injustice branded as slave morality. Nietzsche would reflect on these themes his entire life, seeing slave morality through Christianity, and pitiless nature through Darwin. Nietzsche was revealed to himself through Callicles, and yet Nietzsche never named him, with the exception of a fleeting allusion in his Basel lectures devoted to Plato, not intended for publication.[25] But in the famous passage of the *Zur Genealogie der Moral* (1.11) on the "magnificent blonde beast hunting for prey and victory," Nietzsche rendered implicit homage to Callicles, who had spoken of young lions that society does not succeed in taming.[26] Callicles' haughtiness smacked enough of distinction to predispose him to Nietzsche's *petit bourgeois* veneration.[27]

The return to and revision of Callicles' ideas was a point of arrival for Nietzsche. In his first book, *Die Geburt der Tragödie*, he had felt the need to polemicize with Socrates—a modern Socrates, behind whom lurked the image of Rousseau, the progenitor of the French Revolution and of socialism.[28] A short time later Nietzsche, reevaluating rhetoric, pursued indirectly his polemic with Socrates; though we need to state at once that it was a very different rhetoric from the one that had been theorized (and in part practiced) in the sphere of Athenian democracy.

"Rhetoric is to be used for this one purpose always, of pointing to what is just," Socrates had said at the conclusion of the *Gorgias* (527c). In rhetoric Nietzsche looked for an instrument that would let him reflect "on truth and falsehood outside the context of morality" (*Ueber Wahrheit und Lüge im aussermoralischen Sinne*).[29] This was the title of a brief unfinished study, originating from an ambitious project conceived when he was barely thirty and never concluded, which at one point Nietzsche thought he would entitle

Der Philosoph: Betrachtungen über den Kampf von Kunst und Er-kenntnis (1872–73).[30] These pages, which were published posthumously in 1903, open with a brief fable:

> Once upon a time, in some out of the way corner of the universe which is dispersed into numberless twinkling solar systems, there was a star upon which clever beasts invented knowing. That was the most arrogant and mendacious minute of "world history," but nevertheless, it was only a minute. After nature had drawn a few breaths, the star cooled and congealed, and the clever beasts had to die.

Before the immensity of the cosmos the periods of human history and human pretensions pale into insignificance, Nietzsche continues. If we could communicate with the mosquito, we would discover that even it considers itself the center of the world. But man's pretension to know truth, besides being fleeting, is also illusory. It has its roots in the regularity of language, but "with words it is never a question of truth, never a question of adequate expression; otherwise, there would not be so many languages." Each word arbitrarily generalizes an absolutely specific sensorial experience; every concept contains a forgotten metaphor which has become unconscious:

> What then is truth? A movable host of metaphors, metonymies, anthropomorphisms: in short, a sum of human relations which have been poetically and rhetorically intensified, transferred, and embellished, and which, after long usage, seem to a people to be fixed, canonical, and binding. Truths are illusions which we have forgotten are illusions; they are metaphors that have become worn out and have been drained of sensuous force, coins which have lost their embossing and are now considered as metal and no longer as coins.

"To be truthful," Nietzsche continued, "means to employ the usual metaphors. Thus, to express it morally this is the duty to lie according to a fixed convention, to lie along with the crowd and in a style binding upon everyone [*in einem für alle verbindlichen Stile zu lügen*]."[31]

The term "style," in this context, is revealing. The idea that equally excellent artistic styles cannot be compared with one another goes back at least to Cicero. But through the intersection with such notions as "taste" or "civilization," directly or indirectly tied to the encounter with non-European cultures, this idea had ended up touching even the moral and cognitive spheres.[32] Nietzsche developed the latent relativistic implications of the notion of "style" to undermine a tenacious anthropocentric prejudice. If it is true that the mosquito and the bird perceive the world differently from man, to ask which among these perceptions of the world is more correct is a senseless question, because it refers to nonexistent criteria: "between two absolutely different spheres, as between subject and object, there is no causality, no correctness, and no expression; there is, at most, an *aesthetic* relation."[33] Man's fundamental impulse, to create metaphors, finds its proper culmination in myth and in art. The purpose of culture is art's domination over life, as occurred in ancient Greece.

VI

"What then is truth? A movable host of metaphors, metonymies, anthropomorphisms: in short, a sum of human relations which have been poetically and rhetorically intensified, transferred, and embellished, and which, after long usage, seem to a people to be fixed, canonical, and binding." In the last decades these phrases have summed up the sense of Nietzsche's new interpretation, according to which he would have been the first to have confronted "the philosophical challenge of a radical reflection on language."[34] But this paradoxical posthumous destiny has ended up obscuring the comprehensive significance of the essay "Ueber Wahrheit und Lüge" from which these phrases were taken.

The ideas that were at the heart of these unfinished pages—that language is intrinsically poetic, and that each word is originally a trope—are taken from a book by Gustav Gerber (*Die Sprache als Kunst*, 1871) that Nietzsche used repeatedly, often verbatim, in his own university lectures on rhetoric.[35] But Nietzsche presented these ideas in the framework of a *conte philosophique*.[36] The opening fable almost seems to be written in the spirit of *Operette morali* by Leopardi, a writer whom Nietzsche, that summer of 1873, seems to have had particularly in mind.[37] The discovery of consciousness on the part of the human race is inserted in a cosmic perspective, and thereby rendered ridiculous. Nietzsche's "in the beginning" rings like a parody of the first chapters of Genesis. This interpretation is confirmed by the only passage in which, in a book intended for publication, Nietzsche alluded to "Ueber Wahrheit und Lüge." In the preface to the second volume of *Mensch-*

liches, Allzumenschliches, he spoke of his parting from Schopenhauer's philosophy, to which he had dedicated the third of the *Unzeitgemässe Betrachtungen*. The change in direction, he wrote, had been anticipated in a piece "kept secret" on truth and falsehood, written while he was in the grip of a crisis of moral skepticism which had led him "to criticize and to go more deeply into the prior pessimism." Because even then, Nietzsche observed, "I no longer believed 'in anything,' as people say, not even in Schopenhauer."[38] The ironic allusion to the populace does not seem very appropriate to a skeptical reflection of an abstractly speculative character. In the eyes of the people, whoever "no longer believes in anything" has separated from the religion of his fathers, and no longer believes in God.

VII

"Born in the house of a pastor," Nietzsche said about himself, in one of his numerous autobiographical comments.[39] The son of a pastor, the grandson (on both his father's and mother's side) of Protestant pastors, Nietzsche was destined to become a pastor in his turn. Among his books was a copy of the Bible in Luther's translation that had belonged to his father, who died in 1849, when Friedrich was only five years old. The volume is still extant: on the flyleaf Friedrich wrote his name and a date, "November 1858." He had only recently enrolled in the school at Pforte. There he studied Hebrew and the Old Testament, but with an eye towards classical philology: in a comment from that period he noted that one could study the Torah in the same way that F. A. Wolf had approached the Homeric question, attributing various parts to various authors. At Bonn, where in the fall of 1864 he enrolled in the theological faculty, in addition to taking courses in church history and classical philology, Nietzsche attended the lectures by Konstantin Schlottmann on the Gospel of John.[40] But after a few months, in January 1865, he decided to dedicate himself exclusively to philological studies, a choice that pained his mother and of which she disapproved.[41] At that time Nietzsche explained that his past interest in theology concerned exclusively "the philological aspect of Gospel criticism and the search for New Testament sources." But in another version of this autobiographical reflection, we find a more intimate declaration, almost a confession: "Then I still imagined that history and historical research could give a direct response to certain religious and philosophical questions."[42] These were the questions on God and the world with which the autobiography written six years before ended.[43] On this ironic note, Nietzsche, at the age of twenty-five, seemed to be taking leave of his own adolescence. But it was a leave-taking fraught with ambiguity. The Basel inaugural lecture delivered in May 1869 concluded with a "confession of faith"—the phrase is significant—which proudly reversed Seneca's celebrated dictum: "philosophia facta est quae philologia fuit."[44] Classical philology had replaced New Testament philology as the instrument thought capable of satisfying fundamental religious and philosophical questions. But shortly thereafter Nietzsche began work on a book that was unrelated and hostile, in both form and substance, to academic philology: *Die Geburt der Tragödie* (1872). An instantaneous reaction to it, the violent pamphlet by Wilamowitz *(Zukunftphilologie!)*, accused Nietzsche of ignorance and preconceived distortion of the sources, and, in the end, brutally invited him to change occupations. Factual criticisms accompanied heavy-handed personal allusions: Wilamowitz, a few years Nietzsche's junior, like him had attended Pforte's famous school.[45]

Wilamowitz's attack was published in June 1872. In the months that followed, Nietzsche had to begin to take stock of the impossibility of reconciling academic philology and his philosophical vocation. In September, while preparing his course on rhetoric, he read or reread Gerber's *Die Sprache als Kunst;* there he chanced upon a passage in which the inadequacy of any sort of translation was used to demonstrate the intimately poetic nature of language.[46] Gerber alluded to the celebrated passage in Goethe where Faust weighs, one after the other, the various translations of the word *logos* in the first verse of the Gospel of John, commencing with Luther's version: "Im Anfang was das Wort." In Faust's dissatisfaction, Gerber saw the confirmation of his own ideas: "But Faust knows that *en archē hēn ho logos* does not correspond precisely to 'im Anfang war das Wort.'"[47]

In "Ueber Wahrheit und Lüge" Nietzsche uses the existence of many languages as evidence of the abyss that separates words and things: language cannot give a satisfactory image of reality. Gerber's observation was introduced in an argument intended to demonstrate the fragility of so-called science. It is also possible that "Ueber Wahrheit und Lüge" originated from the impulse to respond to Wilamowitz's philological objections by projecting them against a philosophical horizon. But Gerber's reference to Goethe and to the Gospel of John must have stirred something more profound. It must have been about this time that Nietzsche formed a deep friendship with Franz Overbeck, seven years his senior, he too a professor (of the history of Christianity) at the University of Basel. For a number of years the two resided in the same house. The first of Nietzsche's *Unzeitgemässe Betrachtungen* (dedicated to David Strauss, author of the highly successful *Leben Jesu*), and Overbeck's *Ueber die Christlichkeit unserer heutigen Theologie* were published the same year by Fritzsch, Wagner's publisher.[48] Nietzsche had the two writings bound together, prefacing them with a dedication in verse that called them "a couple of twins coming out of the same nest," children of two fathers and of a single mother: friendship.[49] Possibly even the essay "Ueber Wahrheit und Lüge," which Nietzsche, suffering from eye trouble, dictated to his friend Carl von Gersdorff at Flims in the Grisons in the summer of 1873, preserves an echo of his intense conversations with Overbeck.[50] They might even have touched on the Gospel of John, on which Overbeck had begun to do research that would occupy him for most of his life.[51] The theological, or, better, antitheological, implications of "Ueber Wahrheit und Lüge" (which seem to have eluded the attention of scholars) become comprehensible in light of the fervent intellectual exchange between Nietzsche and Overbeck, who was thoroughly familiar with the texts we are about to discuss.[52]

VIII

The volume that opens the series of Luther's Latin writings in the Erlangen edition contains a sermon, "In Natali Christi," delivered in 1515.[53] Luther was on the eve of the break that would sunder his and so many other lives: a young monk who repeatedly quoted Aristotle and praised his philosophy, calling it "beautiful, even if understood by few, and useful for the highest theology." But he had already arrived at some of the cornerstones of his thought. Why, Luther asked, is Christ, the Son of God, called "Verbum" at the beginning of the Gospel of John? Because, he answered, the first chapter of the Gospel of John admirably clarifies (*miro lumine exponit*) the beginning of Genesis: the Word, who had been with God *ab aeterno*, is the word that creates the world (*Dixit Deus "Fiat" et factum est*).[54] Almost twenty years later, in his commentary on Psalm 45, Luther reiterated the juxtaposition of the two passages implicitly harkening back to his youthful sermon.[55] Luther's biblical exegesis was based on his Trinitarian speculation: the word (*verbum*) is the result of the incarnation of God in Christ as Word (*verbum*).[56] In his sermon "In Natali Christi," Luther distinguished between interior word and exterior word, concluding that the first is enveloped in sounds, in words, in letters, just as honey is enveloped in the honeycomb, the wall in the tiles, the bread pulp in the crust, life in the flesh, and the word in the flesh (*interius illud autem sono, voce, literis est involutum, sicut mel in favo, nucleus in testa, medulla in cortice, vita in carne et verbum in carne*)."[57] Christ, the Word, is truth ("I am the way and the truth," John 14:6): but it is a truth that becomes incarnate in sounds, in letters—and in tropes.

This theme had emerged in Christian exegesis many centuries before when Augustine, imbued with rhetorical doctrine which he had mastered and then taught in his youth, had gone more deeply into that distinction between literal and spiritual interpretation that Origen had placed at the heart of his biblical readings. In a chapter of his *De doctrina christiana* (3.29.41–42), Augustine observed that a knowledge of tropes—allegory, enigma, parabola, and so forth—is indispensable to resolve the apparent ambiguities in the sacred texts.[58] An echo of this recommendation reached from Cassiodorus right through the entire Middle Ages.[59] It recurs insistently in the exegetical works of the Augustinian monk and then ex-monk Martin Luther.[60] With his rich experience as translator, Luther pointed out to his readers the tropes that are scattered in the sacred texts. Christ, he wrote, often resorts to allegories and parables, which, like painted images, move the populace and simple folk;[61] Paul uses allegory—that allegory that only a perfect acquaintance with Christian doctrine permits him to employ without risk—like a great artist (*optimus artifex*), avoiding the excesses of Origen and Jerome.[62] When he speaks of "foreskin" and "circumcision" to designate respectively gentiles and Jews, Paul uses a synecdoche, "an extremely common trope in the sacred literature."[63] In fact, as far as rhetoric is concerned, Paul even surpasses Cicero himself, because (as Luther observes elsewhere) the word of God has a specifically rhetorical dimension: "worldly rhetoricians boast of arranging words in such a way as to give the impression of communicating and making visible the thing itself: this is precisely the characteristic of Paul, that is to say of the Holy Spirit."[64] Luther's understanding of Christ's very redemption of the human race is expressed by means of a trope, the metaphor.[65]

It has been observed that Nietzsche, in the notes for his university course on ancient rhetoric, as well as in his "Ueber Wahrheit und Lüge," neglects rhetoric as effective discourse in order to concentrate on tropes.[66] Today we know that he was turned in this direction by his encounter with Gerber's *Die Sprache als Kunst*, which had put him in contact with idealistic thought on language, from Wilhelm von Humboldt forward.[67] But when Gerber, following Humboldt, wrote that "language is spirit" [*Die Sprache ist Geist*], he was only reformulating the idea expressed by Luther, theologian, exegete, and translator, that the (Holy) Spirit is language: thereby confirming that the philosophy of German idealism is in many respects a secularized (Protestant) Christianity.[68]

The Word that is truth, the Word through which everything that exists has been created, the Word that communicates by means of rhetorical tropes: all of these themes Nietzsche resurrected and overturned in a radically skeptical direction.[69] If everything in language is a trope, if grammar itself is nothing but the product of figures of speech, the pretense to know the world through language is absurd.[70] To Pilate's question—"What is truth" (John 18:38)—Christ had remained silent. Nietzsche reformulated it, and answered: "A movable host of metaphors, metonymies, anthropomorphisms . . ." Nietzsche's opposition to Christianity comes into being here in these pages jealously kept hidden from the public, because they were too weighted down with private allusions and ambivalence: it does not seem too risky to suppose that he had experienced his own separation from the Christian faith as an affront to his father's memory.[71] But the reflections contained in the fragment "Ueber Wahrheit und Lüge" continued to stimulate Nietzsche's published writings, especially *Menschliches, Allzumenschliches*, as well as his notes from the 1880s.[72] One of the many tables of contents of the unfinished book that should have been called *Der Wille zur Macht* opened with a chapter entitled "What Is Truth?"[73]

IX

The echo of "Ueber Wahrheit und Lüge" has endured even outside the strictly philosophical sphere. In the 1970s the fragment became one of the founding texts of deconstructionism, thanks especially to the highly perceptive interpretation Paul de Man devoted to it in an essay originally presented at a Nietzsche conference organized by the journal *Symposium*.[74] One of the participants, Robert Gates, criticized de Man for portraying Nietzsche strictly as an ironic commentator on reality, and the conference for not having taken up political, social, and economic themes. Such subjects as "Nietzsche and Vietnam" or "Nietzsche and Nixon" or "Nixon and Our Value-System," Gates observed, "would be more congenial to his spirit," and he added: "Nietzsche without reference to the Reich is unthinkable to me." De Man responded politely that the attempt, comprehensible from an ethical or psychological perspective, to go beyond an ironic point of view is, however, without "philosophical foundation. Nietzsche gives us no justification to speak of a stage that would be 'beyond' irony. Instead he constantly warns against the illusion of giving in to this desire. It is also from this point of view that we can understand the relevance of Nietzsche with regard to the political questions that you mention."[75]

None among the participants was at the moment in a position to grasp what those words meant to the person speaking them. Between 1940 and 1942 Paul de Man had published a series of articles, some openly anti-Semitic in character, in *Le Soir*, a Belgian collaborationist newspaper—a fact that he carefully kept hidden and that emerged only after his death.[76] Much—too much—has been written about this episode. But it should be noted here that, in spite of the persistence of certain themes, such as the not particularly original one of the autonomy of art, an enormous distance separates those early articles from the essays of de Man's maturity. A close relationship exists, however, between the mask that he wore for forty years and his work as a critic.[77] In 1955, writing from Paris to Harry Levin (one of his academic protectors), de Man spoke of the "long and painful soul-searching of those who, like myself, come from the left and from the happy days of the *Front populaire*."[78] The person voicing this falsehood was the same

as the critic who, a few years later, with unusual warmth presented the work of Borges to an American public and spoke of one
of its recurring themes, "duplicity," in these terms:

> The creation of beauty thus begins with an act of duplicity . . . The duplic-
> ity of the artist, the grandeur as well as the misery of his calling, is a recur-
> rent theme closely linked with the theme of infamy . . . The poetic im-
> pulse in all its perverse duplicity, belongs to man alone, marks him as
> essentially human.[79]

Was de Man speaking about Borges or through Borges? But here we
are still on the relatively simple plane of content. Much more significant is the fact that de Man had reached the point of developing
a critical theory which saw "the act of reading as an endless process in which truth and falsehood are inextricably intertwined."[80]
These words date from 1970. That same year de Man's "The
Rhetoric of Temporality" (which immediately became famous)
marked the rediscovery of rhetoric, but without mention of Nietzsche.[81] Shortly afterward de Man spotted in the essay "Ueber Wahrheit und Lüge im aussermoralischen Sinne" the possibility of giving a more profound interpretation of Nietzsche than he had done
in earlier studies, among which a particularly important one was
"Literary History and Literary Modernity."[82] Baudelaire's modernity, like Nietzsche's, "is a forgetting or a suppression of anterior-
ity," a flight from history that, however, as Nietzsche himself
demonstrated, is condemned to be vanquished: it is impossible
not to perceive in this phrase of de Man's, now that his secret has
been revealed, a sort of autobiographical echo.[83] He would have
been attracted even more by the radical antireferential rhetoric
proposed in "Ueber Wahrheit und Lüge," which reduces truth to a
medley of tropes. But what does all this prove? That critical intelligence can be reinforced by shame, by a sense of guilt, by the fear
of being discovered? De Man's feelings do not concern us, but his
antireferential arguments do. De Man is very careful not to fall
into the ingenuousness of the skeptic who casts doubt on everything but himself. He opts for a perpetually vacillating pendulum
between truth and falsehood: intellectually a more subtle position, but existentially fragile. On one occasion the voice of de
Man, usually so urbane (cuttingly urbane) became strident. Hugo
Friedrich had spoken of the "loss of representation" of the modern
lyric, proposing, de Man commented, "the crudest extraneous and

pseudo-historical explanation of this tendency as a mere escape from a reality which is said to have become gradually more unpleasant ever since the middle of the nineteenth century."[84] Friedrich had touched a nerve. We know today that de Man had many reasons for wanting to free himself from the weight of history. Of course, the exploration of the autonomy of the significant is also born from internal, endogenous stimuli. But as Nietzsche, followed by de Man, observed, even flight from history has to be put into a historical context. An apparently abstract idea such as the antireferential version of rhetoric has taken on, in some eyes, emotive elements, because it offered (or seemed to offer) the possibility of dispelling an unbearable past. Sarah Kofman, who in the early 1970s had published a book filled with the evidence of her own involvement with Nietzsche and the metaphor, took her own life more than twenty years later, after having related her childhood as a persecuted Jewish girl.[85] Reality's revenge in this case was literal and homicidal, not metaphorical and blandly posthumous as in the case of de Man. But to discern the precise distance between these two individual events may cast light on even the unscholarly reasons that, from the mid-1960s, led to reading Nietzsche in a new light. We might begin symbolically with the conference held at Baltimore in 1966 to present to an American academic public the latest findings of French structuralism—or, in the intention of some of the participants, to prepare a dignified funeral for it. Jacques Derrida concluded his own presentation, principally devoted to a critique of the work of Lévi-Strauss, with these words:

this structuralist thematic of broken immediacy is therefore the saddened *negative*, nostalgic, guilty, Rousseauistic side of the thinking of play whose other side would be the Nietzschean *affirmation*, that is the joyous affirmation of the play of the world and of the innocence of becoming, the affirmation of a world of signs without fault, without truth, and without origin which is offered to an active interpretation.[86]

Derrida declared ironically that he did not want to have to choose between these two opposing aspects. In reality, his entire presentation, beginning with its very title ("Structure, Sign and Play in the Discourse of the Human Sciences"), leaned in the direction of Nietzsche and of play.[87] Truth was being liquidated in favor of an active interpretation, namely one without constrictions and limits; the West was being incriminated as logocentric, and contemporaneously it was being absolved in the name of the innocence of becoming proclaimed by Nietzsche.[88] There was enough there to fascinate at the same time both the heirs of the colonizers and the heirs of the colonized.

In this spirit de Man read the famous page of the *Confessions* in which Rousseau feels tormented even decades after he had unjustly accused an innocent woman servant of theft: "it is always possible to face up to any experience (to excuse any guilt), because the experience always exists simultaneously as fictional discourse and as empirical event and it is never possible to decide which one of the two possibilities is the right one." This absolution of Rousseau in Nietzsche's name certainly had, as has been repeatedly noted, unconfessable autobiographical overtones.[89] But the strategy employed had infinitely broader implications. "Rhetoric as innocence," rhetoric as the instrument of individual and collective self-absolution, is the theoretical counterpart of "the rhetoric of innocence" through which, as Franco Moretti observed in the course of analyzing what he defined as "the modern epic form," the West repeatedly absolved its own crimes.[90]

X

"The horror! The horror!" are the last words of Kurtz, the protagonist of *Heart of Darkness*. Edward Said has juxtaposed the multiplicity of narrative points of view used so tellingly by Conrad to Nietzsche's perspectivism, commencing with the usual quotation from "Ueber Wahrheit und Lüge": "What then is truth"?[91] But he observed that Conrad is less radical than Nietzsche. To be sure, in *Heart of Darkness*, as elsewhere, Conrad wants to communicate a cognitive and moral judgment on the story he is recounting *in spite of and through* the multiplicity of narrative view points. (It is this attrition that makes Conrad's project so instructive for today's historian.) But even Nietzsche's skepticism is not unlimited.[92] After having rejected as senseless the question of whether the world perceived by man is more fitting than the world perceived by the mosquito, Nietzsche tacitly postulates the existence of a single world dominated by a ruthless struggle for survival, in which man kills the mosquito and the mosquito transmits malaria to man thereby killing him. The historical world is dominated by an analogous law: the "law of nature" evoked by Thucydides in the dialogue between the Athenians and the Melians. Moralities are plentiful, power is unique: "Diese Welt ist der Wille zur Macht," this world is will to power.

In the places inhabited by Kurtz horror dwells still, but on an incomparably vaster scale. Men, women, and children die by the hundreds of thousands from massacres, epidemics, and famine, surrounded by the blue helmets of the United Nations and observed by television via satellite. Under the eyes of the West the world is indeed becoming one: a world in which homogeneity and cultural diversity, subordination and resistance are inextricably intertwined.[93] To comprehend this process, which began four centuries ago, the relativistic model outlined by Nietzsche does not help much. The supremacy of the so-called developed nations also has cultural roots and depends on the control of reality and its perception. When the plundering of the world by Europeans was still in its infancy, Montaigne branded the exploits of the Spanish *conquistadores* with his famous phrase "mechaniques victoires." There is everything to be learned from Montaigne's emotional and intellectual generosity. But his dismissive tone over the technological supremacy of the Spaniards is not acceptable. The knowledge incorporated into those muskets gave the *conquistadores* the possibility of controlling more efficiently the world that (even if by means of different cognitive categories) they shared with the American natives.[94] To attribute a superior value to the civilization of the *conquistadores* on this basis would be a crude simplification. But their victory is an undeniable fact. The limitation of relativism—whether in the meek and tolerant version, or in the ferocious version—is that it misses the distinction between judgment of fact and value judgment, suppressing, depending on the case, one or the other of the two terms.

XI

That limitation is at once cognitive, political, and moral. A decade or so ago at a conference held at an American university, a well-known scholar expatiated on a thesis dear to him according to which it is impossible to find a rigorous distinction between historical and fictional narrative. In the discussion that followed, a female Indian student exclaimed in anger: "I am a woman, a woman of the Third World, and you are telling me this!" I have thought back to these words reading "Situated Knowledges," an essay by Donna Haraway published in 1988 in the journal *Feminist Studies*. Haraway explicitly warns against mythologizing women of developing countries.[95] But her impatience toward the relativism dominating especially, but not exclusively, the American intellectual scene even has moral roots, which suggest to her these incisive words: "Relativism is a way of being nowhere while claiming to be everywhere equally. The 'equality' of positioning is a denial of responsibility and critical inquiry." On the contrary, Haraway contends, we must embark from a partial, "situated" knowledge to construct a "usable, but not an innocent, doctrine of objectivity." Not innocent, because it is conscious of the existence of "a very strong constructionist argument for *all* forms of knowledge claims, most certainly and especially scientific ones," so that in the sphere of scientific discourse, "artifacts and facts are parts of a powerful art of rhetoric."[96]

To begin from "somewhere" is an honest intention, especially if contrasted with irresponsible relativist ubiquity, but it runs the risk of fragmenting knowledge (and social life) into a series of incommunicable points of view, in which each group is enclosed within its own relationship with the world. Here we rediscover the theme that, alluded to at the start, constitutes the general background of these specialized discussions: that of cohabitation between diverse cultures. Haraway emphasizes translation, which has the advantage of being "interpretive, critical and partial."[97] However, she does not speak of proof. Although she rejects the radically skeptical consequences of the deconstructionist thesis on the "rhetorical nature of truth, including scientific truth," she does not place its premises under discussion and thus ends up imprisoned by them.

Among these premises there is the incompatibility between rhetoric and proof, or (which is the same thing) the tacit acceptance of that nonreferential interpretation of rhetoric which, as we saw, goes back to Nietzsche. I believe, instead, that any discussion about history, rhetoric, and proof must set out from the text that Nietzsche, after he had studied and translated it for his Basel classes, then set aside: Aristotle's *Rhetoric*.[98] The thread linking the apparently heterogeneous themes of the following chapters begins here.

XII

The disrepute into which rhetoric had fallen toward the end of the eighteenth century lasted until just a few decades ago. But the rediscovery of rhetoric, and of Aristotle's in particular, has found small echo in the recent discussions on the methodology of history, for reasons that are implicit in what I have said up to now.[99] The vision of rhetoric prevailing today prevented us from seeing that the writing with which, as we say, the modern critical method begins, namely the demonstration of the false donation of Constantine provided by Lorenzo Valla in the mid–fifteenth century, is based on a combination of rhetoric and proof (chapter 2), or more precisely, on a rhetorical tradition descending from Quintilian, and even further back from Aristotle, in which the discussion of proof played an essential role. Marc Bloch justly believed that the publication of Mabillon's *De re diplomatica* (1681) was "une grande date en vérité dans l'histoire de l'esprit humain." But there could not have been a Mabillon without Valla: a name that does not figure in Bloch's posthumous reflections.[100]

The identification of the trajectory that connects Aristotle to Quintilian, to Valla, to the Maurists and to us has more than historiographical implications. It allows us to reread the *Rhetoric* (chapter 1) beginning with the passage (1357a) in which Aristotle observes, apropos the phrase "Dorieus won the Olympic Games," that no one takes the trouble to clarify that the prize of the Olympic games is a crown, because "everyone" knows this. The most elementary communication presupposes a shared, obvious, and thus unstated knowledge; this may be an apparently casual observation but it has a concealed meaning, revealed by the implicit allusion to a parallel passage in Herodotus. The tacit knowledge evoked by Aristotle is tied to one's belonging to Hellas: the "everyone" is "all the Greeks," and, in fact, Persians are excluded from that knowledge. We know that Greek civilization established itself by standing up against the Persians, and, more generally, against barbarians. But Aristotle also tells us something else, that the discourses analyzed by rhetoric—those spoken in the public squares and in courtrooms—refer to a specific community, not to men as rational animals. Rhetoric moves in the realm of the probable, not in that of scientific truth, and in a circumscribed perspective, far removed from innocent ethnocentrism.

This last expression, intentionally anachronistic, could lead one to think that the theme of premises not being mentioned because they were obvious was confronted beginning only in the eighteenth century, in the course of the deliberations that would lead to the birth of anthropology.[101] This is true for social relations in general. But in the sphere of textual analysis, something closely resembling such a confrontation had begun three centuries earlier, when jurists, antiquarians, and philologists had set themselves to deciphering a Roman law, a fragmentary inscription, a verse from a Latin poet through the reconstruction of lost everyday contexts. When Valla observes that in the alleged donation of Constantine the word *diadema* signifies a "crown" (*corona*) and not, as in classical Latin, a "headband," he transforms Aristotle's observation on a tacit and obvious everyday matter—the crown as the prize in the Olympics—into an instrument of research.[102] The knowledgeable use of context causes the anachronism, written in invisible ink, to emerge.

The voice of the forger (chapter 2) emerges between the lines of the alleged donation of Constantine. In the traces of Aristotle and Valla I have attempted to recapture the voices of the natives of the Marianas in the fictional oration delivered by a person who, according to the Jesuit Le Gobien, was attempting to incite them to revolt (chapter 3). Even in this case rhetoric—a rhetoric based on evidence—was both the object and the instrument of research. It was not my intention to identify a fake, but to demonstrate that the *hors-texte*, what is outside the text, is also *in* the text, nestling in its folds: we have to discover it, and make it talk.[103]

"Make it talk": it is worth the trouble to pause a moment over this expression or others like it, only apparently innocent. In that part of Aristotle's *Rhetoric* dedicated to external or artificial evidence we find, alongside the testimony, the contracts, and the oaths, also torture. It is of course true that Aristotle had no illusions about the latter, applicable only to slaves: "those under compulsion are as likely to give false evidence as true" (1377a). Many centuries later Francis Bacon was more optimistic: nature, he proclaimed, reveals the truth only after it is subjected to the coercion of experimentation, "under constraint and vexed."[104] The analogy proposed by Bacon is still with us, but it has taken on a decisively embarrassing sound: torture is practiced throughout the world, but underhandedly, usually without the shield of legitimacy. It is one sign among many that the content of the word "proof," or of its synonyms, does not exactly correspond to what the word *pistis* meant in the Greece of the fourth century B.C. The thread uniting the two notions is equally clear. Both refer to a sphere of probable truth, which coincides neither with sapiential truth, guaranteed by the person who proposes it and as such beyond proof, nor with the impersonal truth of geometry, entirely demonstrable and accessible to anyone—even to a slave, as Plato demonstrated in the *Meno*.[105] On this point, in spite of appearances, we have not moved much beyond the Greeks.

Even the insistence on the connection between power and knowledge, made popular by Foucault, leads back to Greece: more precisely, through Nietzsche to the Sophists. The inclusion of torture among rhetorical proof seems to exacerbate that link, reducing knowledge to the brutal exercise of power. Naturally this is an unacceptable conclusion, for reasons both of principle and of fact. But in evaluating the evidence historians should remember that every point of view on reality, in addition to being intrinsically selective and partial, depends on the power relations that condition, through the possibility of access to the documentation, the general image that a society leaves of itself. To "brush history against the grain" (*die Geschichte gegen den Strich zu bürsten*), as Walter Benjamin urged, one has to learn to read the evidence against the grain, against the intentions of those who had produced it.[106] Only in this way will it be possible to take into account, against the tendency of the relativists to ignore the one or the other, power relationships as well as what is irreducible to them.

XIII

Walter Benjamin's words quoted above are part of one of his "Theses on the Philosophy of History" (n. 7), which contains an attack on positivist historicism and its pretense to bring back the past through empathic identification. In this connection Benjamin quotes Flaubert ("Peu de gens devineront combien il a fallu être triste pour ressusciter Carthage"). But the novelist Flaubert, even in *Salammbô*, uses more complex instruments than mere empathy. Chapter 4 is dedicated to one of these, once again, the subject of rhetoric, but a visual rather than typographical rhetoric: we could call it a typographical trope of zero degrees. In this case, instead of reading between the lines, I have tried to decipher the blank space that divides two paragraphs of *L'Édu-cation sentimentale.*

The inclusion here of a novelist, even of a very great novelist such as Flaubert, in an essay devoted to history, rhetoric, and proof, seems to unexpectedly corroborate the current skeptical thesis that insists that fictional narratives are comparable to historical narratives. My purpose is precisely the opposite: to oppose the skeptics on their own terrain, demonstrating through an extreme example the cognitive implications of the narrative choices (including those of fictional narrative). Against the rudimentary notion that narrative models intervene in historiographical labors only at the end, to help organize the collected material, I attempt to demonstrate that they play a role instead at every stage of the research, creating both roadblocks and possibilities.[107]

Last century the enthusiasm for scientific and technological progress translated itself into an image of knowledge (including the historiographical) hinging on the passive reflection of reality. In our own century an analogous enthusiasm has emphasized, instead, the active, constructive elements of knowledge. Among the reasons for this success is perhaps above all the possibility offered to part of humankind to make reality appear and disappear with a simple gesture, by flicking the television set on and off. I have already said enough about how this situation can provoke phenomena of subconscious repression. But my disagreement with skeptical relativism should not deceive anyone. The idea that sources, if reliable, offer immediate access to reality, or at least to one face of reality, seems to me equally rudimentary. Sources are neither open windows, as the positivists believe, nor fences obstructing vision, as the skeptics hold: if anything, we could compare them to distorting mirrors. The analysis of the specific distortion of every specific source already implies a constructive element. But construction, as I attempt to demonstrate in the following pages, is not incompatible with proof; the projection of desire, without which there is no research, is not incompatible with the refutations inflicted by the principle of reality. Knowledge (even historical knowledge) is possible.

Notes

1. "Truth in the writing of history has come under fire repeatedly in recent years in relativist interpretations that have sometimes turned history

into little more than rhetoric," G. Bowerstock observed, reviewing a number of polemical commentaries on *Black Athena*, the much discussed best-seller by Martin Bernal ("Rescuing the Greeks," *The New York Times Book Review*, 25 February 1996, p. 7, apropos M. Lefkowitz, *Not Out of Africa* [New York, 1996] and *Black Athena Revisited*, ed. M. Lefkowitz and G. MacLean Rogers [Chapel Hill, 1996]). Such a statement by a well-known historian of antiquity is particularly significant.

2. M. Troper, "The Problem of the Islamic Veil and the Principle of School Neutrality in France" (I should like to thank the author who allowed me to read the text of his unpublished lecture).

3. R. Rorty, "Nietzsche, Socrates and Pragmatism," *South African Journal of Philosophy* 10 (1991):61–63.

4. F. Nietzsche, *Menschliches, Allzumenschliches* 1:92 (Nietzsche, *Werke. Kritische Gesamtausgabe*, ed. G. Colli and M. Montinari, vol. 4, tome 2 [Berlin, 1967], pp. 87–88 [henceforth KGW]).

5. There is a discussion of the various interpretations in H. Herter, "Pylos und Melos" (1954) (reprinted in H. Herter, ed. *Thukydides* [Darmstadt, 1968], pp. 369–99; but see the entire collection). For more up-to-date bibliography, see S. Hornblower, *Thucydides* (London, 1987). The references are taken from R. Warner's translation (Harmondsworth, 1954).

6. Dionysius of Alicarnassus, *On Thucydides*, trans. W. K. Pritchett (Berkeley, 1975), chs. 37–41. The last point is taken up again by W. Nestle, "Thukydides und die Sophistik" (1914), reprinted in *Griechische Studien* (Stuttgart, 1948), pp. 321–73, especially p. 351. On the succession of exchanges in the dialogue, see S. Cagnazzi, *La spedizione ateniese contro Melo del 416 A.C.* (Bari, 1983), but the hypothesis that the dialogue is an independent text inserted by Xenophon is not convincing.

7. See G. E. M. de Ste. Croix, "The Character of the Athenian Empire," *Historia* 3 (1954): 1–41, especially pp. 12–13. After saying that the dialogue of the Melians "is not to be treated as an historical record" (p. 12, n. 13), he contradicts himself: "It is particularly interesting to observe that in 416 the Athenian envoys were not permitted by the Melian authorities to address the assembled people . . . a circumstance upon which Thucydides allows the Athenians to make scornful comments" (p. 13). According to Ste. Croix, Thucydides' revamping was limited to the comments of the Athenians; according to the interpretation being proposed here, it also included the circumstances in which the colloquy took place.

8. It is pointed out naturally by L. Strauss, *Thoughts on Machiavelli* (Glencoe, Ill., 1958), p. 10.

9. On the juxtaposition Thucydides-Plato, see also *Morgenröthe*, 3.168 (KGW V/1 [Berlin, 1971], pp. 150–51); *Götzen-Dämmerung*, "Was Ich den Alten verdanke," par. 2 (KGW VI/3 [Berlin, 1969], pp. 149–50).

10. Thus, according to Nestle, "Thukydides," p. 352: "Die hergebrachte Meinung vertreten die Melier, die Bewohner einer kleinen, unscheinbaren Insel; die harten Gesetze der Wirklichkeit enthüllen die Athener, die Bürger der geistigen Metropole Griechenlands. Auf wessen Seite der Geschichtschreiber die gewichtigere Autorität sieht, kann schon

hiernach, ganz abgesehen von dem Gang der Ereignisse, der den Athenern recht gibt, nicht zweifelhaft sein." Nestle's essay appeared in 1914; it is difficult not to read into these words an allusion to the German invasion of Belgium (even in this instance "the hard law of reality" proved its enthusiastic apologists wrong). On the term "Machiavellianism" used for Thucydides in reference to the dialogue between Athenians and Melians, see the concerns expressed by L. Strauss, *Natural Right and History* (Chicago, 1950, 1953), p. 58 (the implicit allusion is to Weber's *Die Wirtschaftsethik der Weltreligionen: Hinduismus und Buddismus* [1916], now in *Gesamtausgabe* I/20, ed. H. Schmidt-Glintzer [Tübingen, 1996], p. 234).

11. G. De Sanctis, "Postille Tucididee. I. Il dialogo tra i Melî e gli Ateniesi" (1930), now in *Scritti minori* (Rome, 1976), 4:497–505, which confutes the argument in favor of a precocious dating for the dialogue proposed by A. Momigliano, "La composizione della storia di Tucidide," *Memorie della R. Accademia delle Scienze di Torino*, "Classe di Scienze Morali, storiche e filologiche," series 2, tome 67 (1933): 6 ff.; J. de Romilly, *Thucydide et l'impérialisme athénien* (Paris, 1947). I have used the English translation by P. Thody, *Thucydides and Athenian Imperialism* (Oxford, 1963), pp. 273ff. (corrected here and there by the author, who added an appendix). See also H. R. Rawlings III, *The Structure of Thucydides' History* (Princeton, 1981), pp. 247–49 (with references to the preceding bibliography). On the writing of the work, and on its substantial unity, see J. H. Finley, *Three Essays on Thucydides* (Cambridge, Mass., 1967), pp. 118–69. S. Hornblower (*Thucydides* [London, 1987], pp. 136ff.) suggests that bk. 5 is among those last written and left unfinished.

12. Ste. Croix, "The Character of the Athenian Empire"; A. H. M. Jones, "The Athenian Democracy and Its Critics," *The Cambridge Historical Journal* 11 (1953): 1–26. See now the astute study by Z. Petre, "L'uso politico e retorico del tema del tirannicidio," in *I Greci*, ed. S. Settis (Turin, 1997), vol. 2, tome 2:1207–240.

13. See, for example, J. H. Finley, *Three Essays*, p. 42; W. K. C. Guthrie, *A History of Greek Philosophy* (Cambridge, 1975), 4:284. For a contrary opinion, see A. W. Gomme, A. Andrews, K. J. Dover, *A Historical Commentary on Thucydides* (Oxford, 1970), 4:163–64, 174; they, however, place little weight on the dialogical (and more generally textual) element. The following references are taken from the translation by D. J. Zeyl (Indianapolis, 1987).

14. Noted also by Hornblower, *Thucydides*, pp. 122–23. The same theme is fully discussed in the *Protagoras*.

15. This is confirmed by the parallelism between being refuted, defined as "to be delivered from the greatest evil" (*kakou tou megistou*) (458a), and committing the wrong defined as "the greatest of evils" (*megiston tōn kakōn*) (469b).

16. For a somewhat different opinion, see Guthrie, *A History*, 4:298–99.

17. See Plato, *Gorgias*, ed. E. Dodds (Oxford, 1959), p. 266. I do not find convincing G. B. Kerferd, "Plato's Treatment of Callicles in the 'Gorgias,'"

Proceedings of the Cambridge Philological Society 200 (1974): 46–52, according to whom Callicles would appear to be represented as democratic.

18. Plato, *Gorgias*, p. 266 (on *nomos*); p. 268 (on 483e3, with cross-reference to Thucydides 5.105 as "the nearest approach . . . in ancient literature." F. Heinimann, *Nomos und Physis* [Basel, 1945]; W. Kranz, "Das Gesetz des Herzens," *Rhenisches Museum* 94 [1951]: 222ff. But see Nestle, *Nomos*, p. 349, n. 57). The contrast between nature-convention as the source of paradoxes is mentioned by Aristotle, *De sophisticis elenchis* 12.173a7ff. with a reference to Callicles. On this point I follow the interpretation proposed by L.-A. Dorion, "Le statut de l'argument dialectique d'après *Réf. soph.* 11.172a9–15," *Dialogue* 29 (1990): 95–110, especially 107–108.

19. Romilly, *Thucydides*, pp. 362–66, who refers (p. 365 n. 3) to M. Pohlenz and E. Barker, for, and E. Schwartz and Wilamowitz, against. That Plato might have known Thucydides is excluded also by O. Luschnat, Pauly-Wissowa, *Supplementband* 12, col. 1282. None cite the passages discussed above.

20. Hornblower, *Thucydides*, pp. 122ff., takes the analogy back to the dependence of Thucydides and Plato on the thought of Socrates.

21. Ste. Croix, "The Character," p. 14, n. 3, cites *Xen. Hell.* 2.2,3; *Isocr.* 4.100; 12.63.

22. This contextual element is underlined by Guthrie, *A History*, 4:298–99.

23. In another passage, Callicles accuses Socrates of "bringing the discussion around to the sort of crowd-pleasing vulgarities" (482e). Even the final exchange in the *Gorgias* overturns a statement by Callicles: J. de Romilly, *Histoire et raison chez Thucydide* (Paris, 1956), pp. 44ff. And it is not by chance that the dialogue concludes with the name of Callicles.

24. See A. Menzel, *Kallikles: Eine Studie zur Geschichte der Lehre vom Rechte des Stärkeren* (Vienna-Leipzig, 1922), p. 81 (apropos reading Plato).

25. F. Nietzsche, *Vorlesungsaufzeichnungen (WS 1871/72–WS 1874/75)*, KGW II/4, ed. F. Bornmann and M. Carpitella (Berlin and New York, 1995), pp. 113ff.

26. Plato, *Gorgias*, ed. E. Dodds, pp. 12–15 (on Callicles); pp. 387–391 (on Callicles and Nietzsche, with bibliography), which I read upon the advice of Alberto Gajano. See also A. von Martin, *Nietzsche und Burckhardt: Zwei Geistige Welten im Dialog*, 4th ed. (Münich, 1947), p. 253. These pages by Dodds were overlooked in D. Brennecke, "Die blonde Bestie. Vom Mißverständnis eines Schlagworts," *Nietzsche-Studien* 5 (1976): 113–45, who catches the allusion to the lion, but not to the *Gorgias*. Equally off the track is F. Müller, "Die blonde Bestie und Thukydides," *Harvard Studies in Classical Philology* 63 (1958): 171–78.

27. See the letter from E. Rohde to F. Overbeck (1 September 1886), after reading *Jenseits von Gut und Böses*, which had just come off the press: "wissen Sie was ich für Nietzsches spätere Jahre fürchte und vor mir sehe? er wird zum *Kreuze* kriechen, aus Ekel an allem und wegen sein

Veneration alles *Vornehmen,* die ihm immer im Blute steckte, nun aber eine recht unangenehme theoretische Verherrlichung bekommen hat" (F. Overbeck to E. Rohde, *Briefwechsel,* ed. A. Patzer [Berlin and New York, 1990], "Supplementa Nietzscheana," vol. 1, p. 109; a segment of the passage is quoted with slight inaccuracy by A. von Martin, *Nietzsche und Burckhardt,* p. 94). See also F. Overbeck, "Erinnerungen an Friedrich Nietzsche," *Die neue Rundschau* 17, no. 1 (1906): 209–31, 320–30, especially p. 212: "neben ihr [N.] die Affektation des Vornehmen eine der schwächsten, bedenklichsten Eigentümlichkeiten war" (C. A. Bernoulli, *Franz Overbeck,* 1:272). The adjective *"petit bourgeois"* is my addition.

28. See also *Götzen-Dämmerung,* "Streifzüge eines Ungemässen," 48 (KGW VI/3, pp. 144–45).

29. KGW III/2 (Berlin and New York, 1973), pp. 369–84 (English version: "On Truth and Lies a Nonmoral Sense," in *Philosophy and Truth: Selections from Nietzsche's Notebooks of the Early 1870's,* trans. and ed. D. Breazeale (Atlantic Highlands, N.J., 1979), pp. 79ff.

30. KGW III/4, p. 40.

31. "Ueber Wahrheit," pp. 374–75 ("On Truth and Lies," pp. 83–84; I have reinserted the term "Stile," which Breazeale translates as "manner").

32. I have discussed these subjects in "Stile: inclusione ed esclusione," *Occhiacci di legno. Nove riflessioni sulla distanza* (Milan, 1998), pp. 136–70.

33. "Ueber Wahrheit," p. 378: "denn zwischen zwei absolut verschiedenen Sphären wie zwischen Subjekt und Objekt giebt es keine Causalität, keine Richtigkeit, keinen Ausdruck, sondern höchstens ein ä s t h e t i s c h e s Verhalten . . ." ("On Truth and Lies," p. 86).

34. See M. Foucault, *Les mots et les choses* (Paris, 1966), p. 316. This passage is cited in a note to the first French translation of "Ueber Wahrheit und Lüge" (F. Nietzsche, *Das Philosophenbuch—Le livre de philosophe,* ed. A. K. Marietti [Paris, 1969], pp. 250–51). Among the contributions sparked by this translation, see J. Derrida, "La mythologie blanche," *Poétique* 5 (1971): 1–52, especially pp. 7–8, 44–45; and, at quite a different level, P. de Man, "Nietzsche's Theory of Rhetoric," *Symposium* 28 (1974): 33–45, especially p. 39. T. Böning (*Metaphysik, Kunst und Sprache beim frühen Nietzsche* [Berlin, 1988]), in a perspective dominated by the dialogue between Nietzsche and Heidegger, pays considerable attention to the writing of "Ueber Wahrheit und Lüge." On its reception, see the review by R. E. Künzli, "Nietzsche und die Semiologie: Neue Ansätze in der französischen Nietzsche-Interpretation," *Nietzsche-Studien* 5 (1976): 263–88; M. Stingelin, "Die Rhetorik des Menschen," *Nietzsche-Studien,* 24 (1995): 336–43. A partial translation of "Ueber Wahrheit und Lüge" is included, significantly, in *Deconstruction in Context,* ed. M. C. Taylor (Chicago, 1986), pp. 216–19. For one example, among many, of the success enjoyed by the passage cited above, see R. Rorty, "The Contingency of Selfhood," in *Contingency, Irony and Solidarity* (Cambridge, 1989), pp. 23–43, especially p. 27. On the entire question, see the important collection of essays edited by J. Kopperschmidt and H. Schanze, *Nietzsche oder "Die Sprache ist Rhetorik"* (Münich, 1994).

35. G. Gerber, *Die Sprache als Kunst* (Hildesheim, 1961), p. 309 and passim (facsimile reproduction of the 3rd—actually 2nd—edition [Berlin, 1885]). Croce's possible interest in Gerber's ideas is confirmed only partially by the brief allusion in *Estetica come scienza dell'espressione e linguistica generale* (1901; reprint Bari, 1950), p. 510. The importance of Nietzsche's explicit referral to Gerber's book was first grasped by P. Lacou-Labarthe and J.-L. Nancy, "Rhétorique et langage," *Poétique* 5 (1971): 99–130 (translated and annotated writings of Nietzsche); see also P. Lacou-Labarthe, "Le détour," *Poétique* 5 (1971): 53–76; M. Stingelin, "Nietzsches Wortspiel als Reflexion auf Poet(olog)ische Verfahren," *Nietzsche-Studien* 17 (1988): 336–68; A. Meijers, "Gustav Gerber und Friedrich Nietzsche," *Nietzsche-Studien* 17 (1988): 369–90.

36. See P. de Man, "Nietzsche's Theory of Rhetoric," *Symposium* 28 (1974): 33–45, especially p. 43.

37. The initial sentences of "Ueber Wahrheit und Lüge" are given between quotation marks in a text dating from the same period, which also remained unpublished: "On the pathos of truth," one of the "Five prefaces to five unwritten books," which Nietzsche presented to Cosima Wagner Christmas Day 1872 (KGW III/2, pp. 249–54, especially pp. 253–54). The last three sentences in the quotation do not appear in the version that has come down to us. On Leopardi's poetry (*Le Ricordanze* and *A un vincitore nel pallone*) recited by Nietzsche and von Gersdorff, see the latter's letter to Rohde dated 9 August 1873, quoted by E. Förster-Nietzsche, *The Young Nietzsche* (London, 1912), pp. 301–302. "*A se stesso*" (To himself) is cited in a slightly later letter from von Gersdorff: see C. A. Bernoulli, *Franz Overbeck und Friedrich Nietzsche: Eine Freundschaft* (Jena, 1908), 1:115. An allusion to the *Canto notturno* in *Vom Nutzen und Nachteil der Historie für das Leben*, begun immediately after, has been deciphered by O. F. Bollnow, "Nietzsche und Leopardi," *Zeitschrift für philosophische Forschung* 26 (1972): 66–69; cf. M. Montinari, *Nietzsche* (Rome, 1996), p. 120.

38. F. Nietzsche, *Menschliches, Allzumenschliches*, vol. 2 (Berlin, 1967), KGW IV/3, p. 4: "Als ich sodann, in der dritten Unzeitgemässen Betrachtung, meine Ehrfurcht vor meinem ersten und einzigen Erzieher, vor dem g r o s s e n Arthur Schopenhauer zum Ausdruck brachte—ich würde sie jetzt noch viel stärker, auch persönlicher ausdrükken—war ich für meine eigne Person schon mitten in der moralistischen Skepsis und Auflösung drin, d a s h e i s s t e b e n s o s e h r i n d e r K r i t i k a l s d e r V e r t i e f u n g a l l e s b i s h e r i n g e n P e s s i m i s m u s—und glaubte bereits 'an gar nichts mehr,' wie das Volk sagt, auch an Schopenhauer nicht: eben in jener Zeit entstand ein geheim gehaltenes Schriftstück 'über Wahrheit und Lüge im aussermoralischen Sinne.'" D. Breazeale, who grasps the importance of the passage, ends up by denying the existence of a break (pp. xx, xlix). In *Ecce Homo* Nietzsche defined *Menschliches, Allzumenschliches* as "monument of a crisis" (see Montinari, *Nietzsche*, pp. 22–23, 108). But the foundations of that monument had been laid some years earlier.

39. "Ich bin als Pflanze nach dem Gottesacker, als Mensch in einem Pfarrhause geboren" (*Werke*, ed. von K. Schlechta, 3:108).

40. J. Figl, *Dialektik der Gewalt: Nietzsches hermeneutische Religionsphilosophie mit Berücksichtigung unveröffentlichter Manuskripte* (Düsseldorf, 1984), pp. 57ff., 8off. (on Schlottmann); R. Bohley, "Ueber die Landesschule zur Pforte. Materialien aus der Schulzeit Nietzsches," *Nietzsche-Studien* 5 (1976): 298–320.

41. F. Nietzsche, *Sämtliche Briefe, Kritische Studienausgabe* (Berlin, 1986), 2:40 (n. 460, 2 February 1865): "Noch dies: meine Wendung zur Philologie ist entschieden. Beides zu Studieren ist etwas Halbes."

42. "Von der Theologie nahm ich nur genau soweit Notiz, als mich die philologische Seite der Evangelienkritik und der neutestam. Quellenforschung anzog . . . Ich bildete mir nähmlich damals noch ein, dass die Geschichte und ihre Erforschung im Stande sei auf gewisse religiöse und philosophische Fragen eine direkte Antwort geben zu können" (F. Nietzsche, *Werke: Historisch-kritische Gesamtausgabe*, ed. C. Koch and K. Schlechta [Münich, 1940], 5:471. A variant of the same text is printed in ibid. pp. 254–56). C. P. Janz, *Friedrich Nietzsche: Biographie* (Münich, 1978), 1:142, has called attention to these passages.

43. F. Nietzsche, *Werke in drei Bände*, ed. von K. Schlechta (Münich, 1982), 3:110: "Und so entwächst der Mensch allem, was ihn einst umschlang; er braucht nicht die Fesseln zu sprengen, sondern unvermutet, wenn ein Gott es gebeut, fallen sie ab; und wo ist der Ring, der ihn endlich noch umfaßt? Ist es die Welt? Ist es Gott?"

44. F. Nietzsche, "Homer und die klassische Philologie" (1869), KGW II/1 (Berlin and New York, 1982), pp. 247–69, especially pp. 268–69.

45. U. von Wilamowitz-Möllendorff, *Zukunftsphilologie! Eine Erwidrung auf Friedrich Nietzsches Ord. Professors der classischen Philologie zu Basel "Geburt der Tragödie"* (Berlin, 1872). (At pp. 13–14 there are various allusions to their common discipleship at Pforte). See W. M. Calder III, "The Wilamowitz-Nietzsche Struggle: New Documents and a Reappraisal," *Nietzsche-Studien* 12 (1983): 214–54; J. Mansfeld, "The Wilamowitz-Nietzsche Struggle: Another New Document and Some Further Comments," *Nietzsche-Studien* 15 (1986): 41–58. I am grateful to Mordechai Feingold for having suggested to me the importance of Wilamowitz's savage critique for the understanding of "Ueber Wahrheit und Lüge."

46. The first volume of *Die Sprache als Kunst* is recorded among the books borrowed by Nietzsche from the Basel University Library in September 1872: see *Nietzsches Bibliothek* [ed. von M. Oehler], *Jahresgabe der Gesellschaft der Freunde der Nietzsche-Archivs*, 14 (1942): 51. On the date of *Zukunftsphilologie!*, see J. Mansfeld, "The Wilamowitz-Nietzsche Struggle," p. 53, n. 70.

47. G. Gerber, *Die Sprache als Kunst*, 1:259.

48. F. Nietzsche, *Briefe. Mai 1872–Dezember 1874*, KGW II/3 (Berlin and New York, 1978), pp. 135–37: letter to Rohde (Basel, ca. 22 March 1873). See, in general, Bernoulli, *Franz Overbeck und Friedrich Nietzsche: Eine Freundschaft*.

49. F. Overbeck, *Ueber die Christlichkeit unserer heutigen Theologie,* 2nd ed., enlarged (Leipzig, 1903), pp. 17–18: "Ein Zwillingspaar aus einem Haus etc."

50. This hypothesis is not considered by K. Pestalozzi, "Overbecks 'Schriftchen' 'Ueber die Christlichkeit unserer heutigen Theologie' und Nietzsches 'Erste unzeitgemässe Betrachtung: David Strauss. Der Bekenner und der *Schriftsteller,*" *Franz Overbecks unerledigte Anfragen an das Christentum,* ed. von R. Brändle and E. W. Stegemann (Münich, 1988), pp. 91–107.

51. The results of his research, extending over forty years, appeared posthumously: F. Overbeck, *Das Johannesevangelium. Studien zur Kritik seiner Erforschung,* edited from the manuscripts by C. A. Bernoulli (Tübingen, 1911).

52. In an essay dedicated to Heidegger ("Metaphorische Wahrheit," in *Entsprechungen. Gott-Wahrheit-Mensch. Theologische Erörterungen* [Münich, 1980], pp. 103–57) E. Jüngel has outlined a theology based on metaphor, taking his inspiration from Nietzsche's "Ueber Wahrheit und Lüge." Following this path, inevitably he encountered Luther.

53. See *D. Martini Lutheri Opera Latina varii argumenti ad Reformationis historiam inprimis pertinentia,* ed. H. Schmidt (Frankfurt am Main and Erlangen, 1865), 1:41–55. For convenience, I cite from the Weimar edition (henceforth WA) which came out almost twenty years later: *D. Martin Luthers Werke,* vol 1 (Weimar, 1883) (photostatic reprint 1966): *Sermo in Natali Christi* (1515), pp. 20–29. See W. von Loewenich, *Die Eigenart von Luthers Auslegung des Johannes prologus* (Münich, 1960) (Bayerische Akademie der Wissenschaften, philosophical and historical section, Kl., Sitzungsberichte, 1960, Heft 8).

54. WA 1, pp. 22–23: "Dixit Deus 'Fiat,' et factum est. Ex quo textu satis accipitur verbum esse apud Deum, quia cum Deus dixit, sine dubio non erat verbum creatum vel humanum, cum tunc nondum aliqua res vel verbum fuerit creatum, sed per dicere seu verbum Dei coeperunt esse, ipsum autem non coepit et ita consonat id quod dixit: 'In principio erat verbum.'" Luther was echoing Augustine's *In Ioannis Evangelium Tractatus,* 1.11.

55. *M. Luthers Werke,* WA 40, tome 2, *Praelectio in psalmum 45* (1533), pp. 589–90: "testimonia scripturae sunt duplicia; quaedam sumpta sunt a priori, quae manifeste dicunt Christum esse filium Dei et verum ac naturalem Deum, qualia multa sunt in Johanne; quae si quis evertere volet, is sciat, quod scriptura sancta evertenda sint, et non ratione humana. Quid clarius esse potest, quam quod dicit: 'In principio erat verbum,' Item: 'Omnia, quae facta sint, per verbum illud facta sunt' [John 1:1, 3]. Non dicit verbum esse factum, sed quod omnia per verbum facta sunt, ergo ipsum verbum non est factum, sed semper fuit. Sed haec clara sunt et tractata a nobis alibi." See also the *Enarrationes in Genesin (Exegetica opera latina),* ed. C. S. T. Elsperger (Erlangen, 1829), 1:22ff.

56. Here I follow the commentary by E. de Negri, *La teologia di Lutero* (Florence 1967), p. 90, to the passage quoted above of the sermon "In Na-

tali Christi": "A fortunate lexical circumstance also contributed to the so-
lidity of the audacious bridge that spans in a single arch from the first
book of Moses to the Gospel of John. In Greek and Latin, as well as in German, a single word—*Logos, Verbum, Wort*—expresses equally well both
the spoken word, as well as the second person of the Trinity." K. Hagen
came to the same conclusion independently: *Luther's Approach to Scripture as Seen in His "Commentaries" on Galatians 1519–1538* (Tübingen,
1993), p. 18 and passim (at p. x he notes the importance, generally under-
estimated, of Luther's Trinitarian thought).

57. WA 1, "In Natali Christi," p. 29. The expression "nucleus in
testa," the meaning of which is not wholly clear, has a precedent in Vitru-
vius, 6:1.3 ("Insuper ex testa nucleus inducatur . . ."), a writer not mentioned by O. G. Schmidt, *Luthers Bekanntschaft mit den alten Classikern*
(Leipzig, 1883).

58. Migne, *Patrologia Latina*, 34, 80–81: "Troporum cognitio neces-
saria." Cf. R. W. Bernard, "The Rhetoric of God in the Figurative Exegesis
of Augustine," in *Biblical Hermeneutics in Historical Perspective: Studies in Honor of Karlfried Froehlich on His Sixtieth Birthday*, ed. M. S. Bur-
rows and P. Rorem (Grand Rapids, 1991), pp. 88–99, who, surprisingly,
omits E. Auerbach, "Figura" [1944] in *Scenes from the Drama of European
Literature* (New York, 1959), pp. 11–76.

59. B. Smalley, *The Study of the Bible in the Middle Ages* (Notre
Dame, 1970), pp. 22–23 (Cassiodorus).

60. See WA 2, "In epistolam Pauli ad Galatas commentarius. 1519," p.
551: "sancti patres allegoriam grammatice una cum aliis figuris tractant
in sacris literis, sicut abunde docet beatus Augustinus in lib. de doctrina
Christiana." A little later, in the context of a discussion on the quadripar-
tite sense of Scripture, Luther contrasts Augustine to Origen and Jerome.

61. WA 40, tome 1, pp. 652–53.

62. WA 40, tome 1, p. 653. Cf. WA 2, "In epistolam Pauli ad Galatas
commentarius. 1519," p. 557 (apropos *Galatians* 4:27). It should be noted
that Luther moved from an initial rejection of searching out the quadripar-
tite meaning of the Bible (WA 1, pp. 507–508) to a more nuanced position
(WA 2, pp. 550–52): see K. Holl, "Luthers Bedeutung für den Fortschritt der
Auslegungskunst" (1920), in *Gesammelte Aufsätze zur Kirchenges-
chichte* (Tübingen, 1932), 1:544–82, especially pp. 552ff.

63. WA 40, tome 1, "In epistolam Pauli ad Galatas commentarius,
[1531] 1535," pp. 184–85 (apropos *Galatians* 2:7); in the same sense, cf. pp.
68–69. On the synecdoche in Luther, see de Negri, *La teologia*, pp. 85–86.

64. WA 2, "In epistulam Pauli ad Galatas commentarius. 1519," p.
604: "Apud Rhetores seculi gloriosissimum est verba ita ponere, ut in eis
rem ipsam simul observari et geri videas, quod Paulus immo spiritus sanc-
tus proprium habet." Cf. Hagen, *Luther's Approach*, p. 111, although he
speaks of linguistic (rather than rhetorical) characteristics of the Holy
Spirit. The passages quoted by K. Dockhorn move in the same direction:
"Luthers Glaubensbegriff und die Rhetorik," *Linguistica Biblica* 21/22
(1973): 19–39, especially pp. 30ff (paragraph 3.1: "Der Heilige Geist als

Rhetor." In addition: WA 40, tome 1, p. 285 (apropos *Galatians* 2:20): "Paulus suam peculiarem phrasin habet, non humanam, sed divinam et coelestem [etc.]" The comparison with Cicero is in the 1531 commentary to *Galatians* 4:15 (WA 40, tome 1, pp. 639–40).

65. See K. Alfsvåg, "Language and Reality: Luther's Relation to Classical Rhetoric in *Rationis Latomianae confutatio (1521),*" *Studia Theologica* 41 (1987): 85–126, especially pp. 102ff., which stresses vigorously (perhaps excessively) the importance of rhetoric for Luther. On this theme, see R. Breymeyer, "Bibliographie zum Thema 'Luther und die Rhetorik,'" *Linguistica Biblica* 21/22 (1973): 39–44; R. Saarinen, "Metapher und biblische Redefiguren als Elemente der Sprachphilosophie Luthers," *Neue Zeitschrift für systematische Theologie und Religionsphilosophie* 30 (1988): 18–39; Hagen, *Luther's Approach to Scripture.*

66. This is noted astutely by de Man, "Nietzsche's Theory of Rhetoric," p. 34, apropos the notes for the rhetoric course, but without drawing the consequences on the interpretive level.

67. See Meijers, "Gustav Gerber," p. 390. Cf. J. Henningfeld, "Sprach als Weltansicht: Humboldt-Nietzsche-Whorf," *Zeitschrift für philosophische Forschung* 30 (1976): 435–52.

68. Cf. Gerber, *Die Sprache,* p. 288. It should be noted that even A. Meijers has searched for a filter that could explain the surprising influence exercised on Nietzsche by Gerber; she found it in the closeness between the latter and Lange, the author of *Geschichte des Materialismus,* which, however, does not concern itself with language ("Gustav Gerber," p. 389).

69. The importance of Luther's Bible translation on Nietzsche's style has been perceptively noted by S. Sonderegger, "Friedrich Nietzsche und die Sprache," *Nietzsche-Studien* 2 (1973): 1–30, especially pp. 13–14, 27. E. Hirsch's "Nietzsche und Luther" (1921), now in *Nietzsche-Studien* 15 (1986): 398–431, and the appendix by J. Salaquarda (pp. 431–39), with bibliography, do not speak of Luther's exegetical writings.

70. See A. Kremer-Marietti, *Nietzsche et la rhétorique* (Paris, 1992), pp. 118–19.

71. R. Bohley, "Nietzsches christliche Erziehung," *Nietzsche-Studien* 16 (1987): 164–96. According to D. Breazeale, pp. li–lii, Nietzsche abandoned the project of the *Philosophenbuch* because it was incompatible with the forms of antiacademic communication that he adopted beginning with *Menschliches, Allzumenschliches.* But "Ueber Wahrheit und Lüge" hardly appears academic.

72. See *Menschliches, Allzumenschliches* 1:11 (KGW IV/2, pp. 26–27: "Die Sprache als vermeintliche Wissenschaft"); 1:33 (KGW IV/2, pp. 48–49: "Der Irrthum über das Leben zum Leben nothwendig"). See also KGW VIII/1 (Berlin and New York, 1974), pp. 197–98 (Summer 1886–Fall 1887); KGW VIII/2 (Berlin and New York, 1970), pp. 81–82 (Fall 1887). See also the sentence "Wahrheit ist die Art von Irrtum, ohne welche eine bestimmte Art von lebendigen Wesen nicht leben könnte" (quoted by E. Spranger, *Lebensformen,* 2nd ed. [Halle, 1921], p. 193) to which M. Heidegger returned repeatedly in his *Nietzsche* (Frankfurt am Main, 1996),

1:217, 457. Breazeale holds (correctly, in my opinion) that the notes from the 1870s "laid the foundations for the books he [Nietzsche] did eventually write" (*Philosophy and Truth*, p. liii). P. Lacoue-Labarthe, who also was among the first to recognize their importance, ended up by rejecting the idea that they could have had any relationship to his mature work ("Le détour"). Cf. G. Most-T. Fries, <">: Die Quellen von Nietzsches Rhetorik-Vorlesung," in "*Centauren-Geburten.*" *Wissenschaft, Kunst und Philosophie beim jungen Nietzsche*, ed. T. Borsche, F. Gerratana, A. Venturelli (Berlin and New York, 1994), pp. 17–46; E. Behler, "Die Sprach-Theorie des frühen Nietzsches," ibid., pp. 99–111.

73. Cf. KGW VIII/3 (Berlin, 1972), p. 337. The interpretation suggested here converges with one proposed by K. Löwith, "Nietzsche et l'achèvement de l'athéisme," in *Nietzsche aujourd'hui?* (Paris, 1973), 2:207–22.

74. See the already cited essay by de Man, "Nietzsche's Theory of Rhetoric," later collected (but without the summary of the discussion, pp. 45–51) in *Allegories of Reading* (New Haven and London, 1979), pp. 103–118, with the title "Rhetoric of Tropes (Nietzsche)"; additional bibliography can be found in M. Clark, *Nietzsche on Truth and Philosophy* (Cambridge, 1990).

75. *Symposium* 27 (1974): 47–49.

76. P. de Man, *Wartime Journalism*, ed. W. Hamacher, N. Hertz, T. Keenan (Lincoln, 1988). See the precise reconstruction by D. Lehman, *Signs of the Times: Deconstruction and the Fall of Paul de Man* (London, 1991) (with full bibliography).

77. See J. Loesberg, *Aestheticism and Deconstruction: Pater, Derrida, and De Man* (Princeton, 1988), pp. 190–200, especially p. 193 (but to reduce the deconstructionism of the mature de Man to an "alibi" is simplistic).

78. P. de Man, *Critical Writings, 1953–1978*, ed. and with an introduction by L. Waters (Minneapolis, 1989), pp. lxv–lxvi (especially p. lxv, n. 5), which reprints, without commenting on it, the letter (dated Paris, 6 June 1955) from de Man to Harry Levin. It should be remembered that in January of that year, as a consequence of a now lost anonymous letter that accused him of collaborationism, de Man had written to Renato Poggioli, codirector of the Society of Fellows at Harvard, alluding with extreme reticence, and in part falsely, to the articles written for *Le Soir* (see Lehman, *Signs*, pp. 198ff, who publishes the letter to Poggioli and discusses it fully). De Man obviously believed that his own past, or, better, the version of it that he had given, was known to Harry Levin, who at the time (as Lehman informs us, *Signs*, p. 193) was codirector of the Society of Fellows with Poggioli.

79. De Man, *Critical Writings*, pp. 123–29: "A Modern Master: Jorge Luís Borges," especially pp. 125, 126, 128).

80. P. de Man, *Blindness and Insight*, 2nd ed. (Minneapolis, 1983), p. ix (the preface is dated 1970).

81. Ibid. pp. 187ff.

82. Ibid, pp. 142–65.

83. This was noted by Lehman, *Signs of the Times*, p. 187; my conclusions differ in part.

84. De Man, *Blindness*, p. 172.

85. S. Kofman, *Nietzsche et la métaphore* (Paris, 1972); S. Kofman, *Rue Ordener, rue Labat* (Paris, 1994). A bibliography of her writings on Nietzsche can be found in *Nietzsche-Studien* 25 (1996): 445–48.

86. J. Derrida, *L'écriture et la différence* (1967; reprint, Paris, 1994), pp. 409–428, especially p. 427: "Tournée vers la présence, perdue ou impossible, de l'origine absente, cette thématique structuraliste de l'immédiateté rompue est donc la face triste, *négative*, nostalgique, coupable, rousseauiste, de la pensée du jeu dont l'*affirmation* nietzschéenne, l'affirmation joyeuse du jeu du monde et de l'innocence du devenir, l'affirmation d'un monde de signes sans faute, sans vérité, sans origine, offert à une intérprétation active, serait l'autre face" (translated in *Writing and Difference* [London, 1978], p. 292). Cf. C. Norris, *Derrida* (London, 1987), pp. 138–41, and W. B. Leitch, *Deconstructive Criticism* (New York, 1983), p. 37, who observes: "we may read this passage as the historic charter of contemporary deconstruction."

87. This is denied by Loesberg (*Aestheticism*, pp. 90–91) with captious and unconvincing arguments.

88. J. Derrida, *De la grammatologie* (Paris, 1967).

89. De Man, *Allegories of Reading*, p. 293. Cf. Loesberg, p. 193, with bibliography (to which should be added Lehman, *Signs*, pp. 216–19).

90. See F. Moretti, *Opere mondo: Saggio sulla forma epica dal "Faust a Cent'anni di solitudine"* (Turin, 1994), p. 51: "Rhetoric as innocence; history as metaphor of geography. I have spoken about these constructions emphasizing their social utility: their ideological function. But what sort of ideologies are these? Who has ever heard speak of them? No one, I'm sure, *and they are interesting precisely for this reason*" (see also pp. 48–52 and passim). (I have not been able to consult the English translation of this work.) Instead, we have had our fill of talk about anti-referential rhetoric assimilated to history: this complements, confirming it, Moretti's thesis (who at p. 50 quotes a passage from Nietzsche's *Vom Nutzen und Nachteil der Historie für das Leben*).

91. E. Said, "Conrad and Nietzsche," in *Joseph Conrad: a Commemoration*, ed. N. Sherry (London, 1976), pp. 65–76, especially p. 67 (the passage is quoted in a slightly different translation).

92. See M. Clark, *Nietzsche on Truth*, pp. 63–93, who, however, adopts a different line of argument. What I have proposed here takes into account the confutation of relativism proposed by E. Gellner, *Cause and Meaning in the Social Sciences* (London, 1973), pp. 50–77, especially p. 66 (cf. A. B. Spitzer, *Historical Truth and Lies about the Past* [Chapel Hill, 1996], p. 57).

93. No one has understood this better than Sebastiâo Salgado, the photographer.

94. T. Todorov, *La conquête de l'Amérique* (Paris, 1982), is an indispensable point of departure.

95. D. Haraway, "Situated Knowledges. The Science Question in Feminism and the Privilege of Partial Perspective," *Feminist Studies* 14 (1988): 575–99; at p. 586 we have an ironic allusion to the "search for the

fetishized perfect subject of oppositional history, sometimes appearing in feminist theory as the essentialized Third World Woman." I should like to thank Nadine Tanyo who suggested that I should read this essay.

96. Haraway, "Situated Knowledges," pp. 584, 582 (with an allusion to Nagel, *A View from Nowhere*). I have discussed these themes in "Distanza e prospettiva: due metafore," *Occhiacci di legno*, pp. 171–93.

97. Haraway, "Situated Knowledges," p. 589.

98. *Vorlesungsaufzeichnungen*, KGW II/4, pp. 523–28 (introduction); pp. 533–611 (translation). See also C. P. Jantz, "Friedrich Nietzsches akademische Lehrtätigkeit in Basel 1869—1879," *Nietzsche-Studien* 3 (1974): 202.

99. See C. Perelman and L. Olbrechts-Tyteca, *Traité de l'argumentation. La nouvelle rhétorique* (Paris, 1958).

100. See M. Bloch, *Apologie pour l'histoire*, preface by G. Duby (Paris, 1974), p. 77, within a section entitled "Esquisse d'une histoire de la méthode critique," which begins by mentioning the donation of Constantine (but not the subsequent demonstration of its falsity).

101. It suffices to think of such texts as Diderot's *Supplément au voyage de Bougainville* (in regard to sexual relations) or Rousseau's *Discours sur les origines de l'inégalité* (in regard to property).

102. See L. Valla, *De falso credita et ementita Constantini donatione*, ed. W. Setz (in the appendix to his *Lorenzo Vallas Schrift gegen die Konstantinische Schenkung.* Bibliothek des Deutschen Historischen Instituts in Rom, vol. 44 (Tübingen, 1975), p. 28.

103. I have been working in this direction from the time of my *I benandanti* (1966); see, especially, "The Inquisitor as Anthropologist," in *Clues, Myths and the Historical Method* (Baltimore, 1989), pp. 156ff. The reference is to Derrida's well-known phrase "Il n'ya pas de hors-texte."

104. F. Bacon, *De sapientia veterum*, XIII: "Proteus, sive materia" (*The Works of Francis Bacon*), ed. J. Spedding et al., 13 [London, 1860], pp. 17–19). J. C. Briggs (*Francis Bacon and the Rhetoric of Nature* [Cambridge, Mass., 1989], pp. 193ff.) notes that evidence is lacking in Bacon's definition of rhetoric. This seems a somewhat superficial opinion in light of what has been said. There are useful observations in P. duBois, *Torture and Truth* (New York, 1991).

105. M. Detienne, *Les maîtres de vérité dans la Grèce archaïque* (1967; reprint, Paris, 1994).

106. W. Benjamin, "Ueber den Begriff der Geschichte," in *Gesammelte Schriften*, vol. 1, tome 2, ed. R. Tiedemann and H. Schweppenhäuser (Frankfurt am Main, 1978), p. 697.

107. The contradictory reactions to my research, which is seen alternately as favorable and hostile to "postmodern" historiography are certainly symptomatic of the field's blurred borders, as P. Schöttler observes: "Wer hat Angst vor dem 'linguistic turn'?," *Geschichte und Gesellschaft* 23 (1997): 134–51, especially p. 145. But underlying these contradictory viewpoints, there is, unquestionably, a misunderstanding of the decisive point indicated above.

1 Aristotle and History, Once More

I

The title of this chapter has two apologetic implications. First, the decision to deal with a text that has been analyzed over and over by generations of interpreters is in itself ambitious; second, being neither a classicist nor a historian of Greek philosophy, I have no specific credentials to do so. Nevertheless, any reflection on the meaning of historiography both for Greeks and for ourselves must necessarily start with the remark made by Aristotle in the ninth chapter of his *Poetics* (1451b). Poetry, he said, is "something more scientific and serious than history." The former is represented by events "either likely or necessary," the latter, by events both specific and real ("what Alcibiades did or what was done to him").[1] In commenting on this famous passage Moses Finley wrote: "He [Aristotle] did not jibe at history, he rejected it."[2] These are uncompromising words, as one could expect from Finley, but they probably need some qualification. This will be an effort to demonstrate that the work in which Aristotle dealt most extensively with historiography, or at least with those essentials that are in a sense close to our own, is not the *Poetics* but the *Rhetoric*.

This statement may immediately cause a misunderstanding. The reduction of historiography to rhetoric has been a crucial (even *the* crucial) weapon in the attack against positivism that has raged in the last thirty years. Although the basic inspiration of this enterprise was ultimately provided by Nietzsche, this approach is today usually associated with the names of Roland Barthes and Hayden White.[3] Their respective points of view are quite divergent, but they share a more or less explicit set of assumptions, which can be described as follows: the fundamental aim of both historiography and rhetoric is effectiveness, not truth; both historians and rhetoricians attempt to convince their audience; the historian's work creates, as a novel does, a self-contained textual world, whose relationship with extratextual realities cannot be submitted to a rigorous examination; both historical and fictional texts are self-referential in so far as they share a common rhetorical dimension.

Within this theoretical perspective, rhetoric, with its aims and limits, plays a crucial role. But which rhetoric? Certainly not the one analyzed in the most famous of the ancient treatises on the subject, Aristotle's *Rhetoric*. A quick glance at its beginning will be sufficient. After having written that "rhetoric is a counterpart of dialectic," and that everybody uses it albeit by chance or by habit, Aristotle clarifies the divergence between his approach and his predecessors':

Now, previous compilers of "Arts" of rhetoric have provided us with only a small portion of this art, for proofs are the only things in it that come within the province of art; everything else is merely an accessory. And yet they say nothing about enthymemes which are the body of proof, but chiefly devote their attention to matters outside the subject; for the arousing of prejudice, compassion, anger, and similar emotions has no connexion with the matter in hand, but is directed only to the dicast. (1.1.3)

The tone of this remark is unambiguous. Aristotle rejects both the attitude of the sophists, who had praised rhetoric as a technique aiming to convince through the motion of affects, and the attitude of Plato, who in his *Gorgias* had condemned rhetoric for the same reason.[4] Contrary to both of them, Aristotle detects a rational core within rhetoric: proof, or rather, proofs. Here we find the connection between historiography, as it has been conceived in modern times, and rhetoric, as it was interpreted by Aristotle—although, it will soon be apparent, his notion of "proofs" was different from ours.[5]

II

Aristotle enumerates three sorts of rhetoric: deliberative, epideictic (that is, aiming either to blame or to praise), and judiciary. Each of them corresponds respectively to a different temporal dimension: the future, the present, and the past (1.1.3). Proofs can be divided into "artificial" and "non-artificial." Among the latter Aristotle mentions "witnesses, tortures, contracts, and the like" (1.2.2); a list that speaks (among other things) of a society that, like Athens in the fourth century B.C., heavily relied on written evidence.[6] There are two sorts of technical proofs: the example (*paradeigma*) and the enthymeme (which are the counterparts, for rhetoric, of induction and *syllogismos* in the realm of dialectic). The example and the enthymeme are related, respectively, to deliberative and judiciary rhetoric; the amplification, on the other hand, is closer to epideictic rhetoric:

> Examples are most suitable for deliberative speakers, for it is by examination of the past that we divine and judge the future. Enthymemes are most suitable for forensic speakers, because the past, by reason of its obscurity, above all lends itself to investigation of causes and to demonstrative proof. (1.9.41)

The implications of this remark emerge in a further passage dealing with enthymemes. Here the reference is to the trial, to the clash between defendant and accuser in court: "The material of enthymemes," Aristotle writes (2.25.8), "is derived from four sources—likelihood [*eikos*], example [*paradeigma*], necessary sign [*tekmērion*], and sign [*sēmeion*]." The accuser is in a difficult situation: his conclusions can be easily rejected, in so far as they are related to what takes place "in the majority of cases" (*epi to poly*). But, being based on a conclusion that is "likely" and not "necessary," their confutation is only apparent. Even enthymemes based on examples and signs are related to the realm of likelihood (2.25.12). Only enthymemes based on necessary signs (*tekmēria*) can lead to conclusions that are beyond refutation (2.25.14; 1.2.16).

The enthymeme, the most important of the technical proofs, is based, Aristotle writes, on a smaller number of premises than is the *syllogismos*. In the latter case, "if any one of these is well known, there is no need to mention it, for the hearer can add it himself."[7] This is followed by an example: "For instance, to prove that Dorieus was the victor in a contest at which the prize was a crown, it is enough to say that he won a victory at the Olympic games; there is no need to add that the prize at the Olympic games is a crown, for everybody knows it" (1.2.13). This, for several reasons, is a perplexing passage.

III

The traditional definition of enthymeme as an abbreviated syllogism is usually related to the *Prior Analytics* 2.27, which reads: "An enthymeme is an incomplete *syllogismos* from likelihoods or signs." In an impressive essay M. F. Burnyeat has shown that the word *atelēs* (incomplete), which exists in a single manuscript, came from an ancient gloss, which at a certain point was incompletely erased from the manuscript. The gloss was the consequence of a Stoic misunderstanding of Aristotle's theory of the enthymeme, which is the main topic of Burnyeat's analysis.[8] But the traditional interpretation of enthymeme as an incomplete or abbreviated syllogism appears to be supported by the aforementioned passage on Dorieus (*Rhetoric* 1.2.13), whose purpose is precisely to illustrate the definition of the enthymeme as a *syllogismos* based on fewer, sometimes undeclared, premises than normal. Burnyeat sees the difficulty, but attempts to overcome it by claiming that in the passage on Dorieus "the argument is not in a syllogistic form, which would require fairly strenuous recasting." But the equivalent syllogism Burnyeat then provides ("All victors at the Olympic Games are winners of crowns; Dorieus is a victor at the Olympic Games; therefore, Dorieus is a winner of crowns") does not seem particularly strenuous.[9] Aristotle's definition of the enthymeme as an incomplete *syllogismos* seems therefore inescapable. But Burnyeat rejects it as absurd:

There is no more logical interest or utility in grouping together arguments that are incompletely expressed that there would be in grouping together arguments that are over-elaborately expressed, or arguments that are obscurely or wittily expressed. A logic of incompletely expressed reasoning is as redundant as a logic of indignant reasoning.[10]

This remark is unconvincing. In saying that in the enthymeme a well-known premise does not need to be mentioned, Aristotle places himself, as we would say today, in an anthropological, not a logical perspective—or, more precisely, in the perspective of rhetoric, which always refers to a concrete, and therefore circumscribed community. Admittedly, although the unspoken premise of his enthymeme, the fact "that the prize at the Olympic games is a crown," does not need to be mentioned "for everybody knows it" (gignōskousi gar pantes), here "everybody" actually means every Greek, not every rational being. This is proven by Aristotle's implicit allusion to Herodotus 8.26, which has apparently been missed by the interpreters of *Rhetoric* 1.2.13.

After his victory at Thermopylae, Xerxes asked a group of Arcadian defectors what the Greeks were doing. The Arcadians replied that they were "keeping the Olympic festival and viewing sports and horse races." Xerxes then asked

> what the prize offered was, and what they contended for; and they told him of the crown of olive that was given to the victor. Then Tigranes son of Artabanus uttered a most noble saying (but the king deemed him a coward for it); when he heard that the prize was not money but a crown, he could not hold his peace, but cried: "Zounds, Mardonius, what manner of men are these that you have brought us to fight withal? 'Tis not for money they contend but for the glory of achievement!"[11]

The point of the anecdote is clear. Only a barbarian could be ignorant of the meaning of the crown, the prize of the Olympic contest, which periodically reaffirmed Greek cultural unity. Only a Greek orator addressing himself to a Greek audience, Aristotle suggested, did not need to mention that the prize of the Olympic contest was a crown. The example became a commonplace. *Anacharsis*, the dialogue by Lucian of Samosata, tells the story of a stranger—a barbarian, a Scythian—who, having watched the games in a Greek gymnasium, questions Solon, the Greek, about them; he starts to laugh when he learns that the prizes are wreaths of olive or pine.[12]

The prize of the Olympic games was just one of the innumerable rules that were written in invisible ink on the fabric of Greek everyday life. Such rules exist in all societies; in a sense, they make societies work. Since antiquity, and until some decades ago, historians were uninterested in those rules: they took them for granted and they often still do. In the aforementioned passage Aristotle alluded to them as unspoken premises, which (as Burnyeat remarks) are *not* a necessary part of the enthymeme: as we have seen, Aristotle simply says, "*if* any one of these is well known, *there is no need* to mention it, for the hearer *can* add it himself" (1.2.13, emphasis added).

IV

But is the Dorieus example an enthymeme? According to one interpreter, Eugene E. Ryan, "the example seems to be one in

which merely a factual statement is advanced, not an enthymeme
. . . what could one be aiming to prove with those words, or about
what could he be attempting to convince? . . . even if this were an
argument, it is hard to see how it would be one that is in some way
rhetorical."[13] This perplexity is understandable, but arguably
groundless.

Aristotle published his *Rhetoric* in approximately 350 B.C. Dorieus of Rhodes, son of Diagoras, had won the Olympic games
three times, in 432, 428, and 424; in 412–407 he had supported the
Spartans.[14] To use an example of an individual who had lived
nearly a century before might seem a bit odd in a section on judicial rhetoric. True, Aristotle wrote that "enthymemes are most
suitable for forensic speakers, because the past, by reason of its obscurity, above all lends itself to investigation of causes and to de-
monstrative proof" (1368a). But a reference to a distant event like
Dorieus's victory would appear to be more appropriate to other
forms of inquiry about the past, such as history. After all, the very
concept of historical time, as opposed to a vague mythical past,
emerged in Greece with the reconstruction of the lists of Olympic
winners, which provided a chronological framework for all sorts of
events.[15] In a typical passage (which incidentally refers to the
same individual mentioned by Aristotle), Thucydides wrote (3.8):
"it was the Olympiad in which Dorieus the Rhodian won his second victory."

Aristotle's erudite works are now lost. Besides preparing a list
of the winners of the Pythian games, he revised and corrected a list
of winners of the Olympic games (such as Dorieus) which had
been worked out by Hippias, the famous philosopher and rhetorician.[16] According to the sarcastic self-presentation which Plato ascribed to him, Hippias boasted about the success he had achieved
speaking in Sparta, saying that "they are very fond of hearing
about the genealogies of heroes and men . . . and the foundations of
cities in ancient times and, in short, about antiquity in general"
(*Hippias Major* 285d).[17] Besides being a rhetorician and a philosopher, Hippias was an archaeologist, or, as we would say today, an
antiquarian.[18] Many years ago Arnaldo Momigliano remarked that
Hippias's erudite works, mostly based on epigraphic evidence, implied "a rationalistic attitude and a critical approach as well."[19]
Aristotle the antiquarian, who continued Hippias's work, can help
us to understand Aristotle the philosopher, who, by submitting
the vocabulary of proof to a close theoretical scrutiny, equated the

rational core of rhetoric with proof. In the same years in which he was revising his treatise on *Rhetoric*, Aristotle deciphered epigraphs—an eminently inferential activity—in Olympia and Delphi in an effort to fix the chronology of the Olympian games' winners.[20] The factual statement "Dorieus won a victory at the Olympic games," being based on a series of inferences "from likelihoods or signs," fulfilled the definition of enthymeme provided in *Rhetoric* 1.2.13.

V

In a perceptive essay, G. E. M. de Ste. Croix analyzed a series of passages taken from Aristotle's works, trying to prove that he read Thucydides, but he was unable to reach a conclusive finding.[21] Ste. Croix focused especially on the expression *to hōs epi to poly* (the "as a general rule," used as a noun) which he traced through several of Aristotle's scientific writings; he did not scrutinize the treatise on *Rhetoric*. In the passage in *Rhetoric* (2.25.8) dealing with the sources of the enthymeme, the expression *epi to poly* (not used as a noun, and much more common) surfaces four times, each instance connected to terms in which Thucydides expressed his cognitive relationship with the past: *eikos, paradeigma, sēmeion, tekmērion.*[22] Let us focus on *tekmērion* which, with the related verb *tekmairomai*, recurs twice, in quick succession, at the very beginning of Thucydides' work. Thucydides starts by saying, in the third person, that the Peloponnesian war he will deal with is the biggest event that ever took place, "inferring this" (*tekmairomenos*) from a survey of the present situation of Greece, as well as from an inquiry about the past constructed "from evidence" (*tekmēriōn*) which he regards as reliable (1.1.1). A few paragraphs later, we read that the best evidence (*tekmērioi de malista*) for the late emergence of the name "Hellenes" is provided by its absence in the poems of Homer (1.3.3). In the so-called archaeological section, the image of ancient times based on proofs (*tōn . . . tekmēriōn*) is opposed to the image, based on fabulous elements (*to mythōdes*), provided by poets and logographers (1.21.1; see also 1.20.1).[23] The conjectural identification of the most ancient section of Athens with the Acropolis and the southern part of the city, based on the temples located in that section, is introduced by the expression *tekmērion de,* "and the proof is this" (2.15.4). In the description of the plague in Athens, the same words, *tekmērion de,* are followed by a remark on the exceptional character of the pestilence, based on the disappearance of birds accustomed to feeding on corpses (2.1.2).

One may wonder whether Aristotle's distinction between proof (*sēmeion*) and necessary proof (*tekmērion*), albeit explicitly referring to judicial rhetoric, could not have been triggered by the loose way in which Thucydides, among others, had used those terms.[24] A few instances will suffice. Thucydides interpreted the custom of bearing arms in Locris, Aetolia, and so forth, as evidence that in the past the same usage was spread everywhere (1.6.2). He advanced a similar argument in the aforementioned passage in which he took the present distribution of temples in the Acropolis as evidence for the location of the city's most ancient section (2.15.3). In both cases Thucydides spoke of proof: but in the former he used the word *sēmeion,* in the latter *tekmērion.* According to Aristotle's terminology, the latter term should be reserved to links which, being both natural and necessary, allow the formulation of a proper natural *syllogismos*: if a woman's breasts are swollen with milk, the woman has begot a child (1.2.18). Thucydides, on the contrary, used a word like *tekmērion* more or less as a synonym of *sēmeion,* in order to describe non-necessary conclusions, valid *epi to poly.*

VI

These remarks throw some unexpected light on the famous passage of the *Poetics* with which we started (1451b), in which Aristotle compared history unfavorably to poetry. But we should remember that Aristotle's *historia* was not identical with our notion of history. In his last book Finley remarked that archival research, which for the Greeks was connected more to "archaeology" or antiquarian research, than to historiography in the proper sense of the word, had been started by the disciples of Aristotle.[25] In the aforementioned passage of the *Poetics* the word "history" (*historia*) is taken from Herodotus, whom Aristotle in his *Rhetoric* (3.9.2) takes to task for his old-fashioned style.[26] Thucydides (especially Thucydides the archaeologist), who repeatedly used arguments based on enthymemes, "which are the body of proof" (*Rhetoric* 1.1.3), might have appeared to Aristotle to be a different and less problematic case.[27]

Archaeology, or antiquarianism, aiming to reconstruct events on the basis of purely indirect evidence, implied an intellectual approach quite different from historiography. Momigliano compared Thucydides' archaeological conjectures to Xenophanes' paleontological conjectures.[28] Xenophanes used *typoi*—traces of shells, fish, seals, or bay leaves found on rocks—as evidence of a very ancient stage in the earth's history.[29] Thucydides interpreted either the disposition of tombs or the diffusion of customs in certain regions as evidence (*tekmēria*) of phenomena that had taken place in Hellas during the ancient past. In both cases the invisible was inferred from the visible, based on discernible traces. Spoken Greek preserved in these words (as happens with many modern languages) the echoes of an ancient venatory knowledge. In Sophocles' *Oedipus Tyrannus* the word *ichnos* (trace), and an adjective related to *tekmairō* resonate in Oedipus's response to the news that the pestilence at Thebes originated in the killing of Laius: "Where is it to be found this obscure trace of an ancient crime?"[30]

We suggested earlier that Aristotle in his *Rhetoric* implicitly referred to historiography (or to its basic core) in a sense that is still familiar to us. This "basic core" might be formulated as follows:

(a) human history can be reconstructed on the basis of traces, clues, *sēmeia*;

(b) these reconstructions imply a series of connections, both natural and necessary (*tekmēria*) which can be regarded as certain: up to now, until somebody proves the opposite, a human being cannot live two hundred years, or be in two different places at the same time, and so forth;

(c) outside that sphere of natural connections, historians deal with what is likely (*eikos*), sometimes with what is infinitely likely. They never deal with certainty, although in historians' writings the distinction between "infinitely likely" and "certain" tends to collapse.

What is the exact meaning, somebody asked, of the expression *hōs eikos* used by Thucydides: does it mean natural? or likely?[31]

These doubts are probably misplaced: from Thucydides' time until today historians have tacitly filled the gaps in their evidence with what is (or what they regard as) natural, self-evident and therefore certain.[32]

Santo Mazzarino, the Italian historian of antiquity, wrote that Aristotle's remark in his *Rhetoric* (1.4.13) that *historiai* belong (and are useful) to politics, not to rhetoric, is "extremely important."[33] But the meaning of that remark becomes clear only if it is placed in context: an analysis of the sphere of *eikos* focused on proof, and particularly on the technical proof based on enthymeme. Burnyeat observed that Aristotle's more relaxed definition of enthymemes from signs included "such indispensable forms of reasoning as 'inference to the best explanation' (in older parlance, inference from effect to cause), without which not only rhetoric and public deliberation, but medicine too, would be severely curtailed."[34] Can we add history to this list? Yes and no. The judicial orator who reconstructed an event of the past by scrutinizing clues and witnesses was closer to Thucydides the archaeologist (and to Aristotle the antiquarian) than to Herodotus, a historian who was not particularly concerned either with proofs or with enthymemes.

VII

All this suggests that in Greece, during the fifth century B.C., rhetoric, history, and proof were closely intertwined. Let us spell out some implications of this remark:

A. The languages we speak are full of words of Greek origin. But the Greek-based words that are at the center of contemporary life, like "economy" and "democracy," are far from being synonyms of their Greek counterparts, as Moses Finley taught us. The same must be said about "history." Nearly half a century ago, in his fundamental essay "Ancient History and the Antiquarian," Momigliano demonstrated that the linguistic continuity between "history" and *historia* conceals a deep discontinuity in their respective content. Historiography, in the modern sense of the word, first emerged in the mid-eighteenth century with the work of Edward Gibbon, as a fusion between two heterogeneous intellectual traditions: philosophical history à la Voltaire and antiquarianism.[35] Momigliano showed that Gibbon's approach had been prepared by the debate between neopyrrhonists and antiquarians that had raged some decades before: the former attacking history on the basis of the contradictions detected in the work of ancient historians, the latter rescuing it through a rigorous scrutiny of primary, mostly nonliterary evidence, such as coins, inscriptions, and monuments. Although Momigliano dealt extensively with the Greek and Roman "archaeological" tradition, the main heroes of his essay were late-seventeenth- and early-eighteenth-century antiquarians. Thucydides' "archaeology" was mentioned by Momigliano only in order to stress how different presumably it was from Hippias's archaeology. My focus on proof leads to a much greater emphasis on Thucydides' bold use of archaeological or literary clues as evidence for a conjectural reconstruction of a distant past. Someone might object that Thucydides, disguised in the past as a late-nineteenth-century German professor, seems to appear now in a different garb, as a late-nineteenth-century English detective or Italian connoisseur. Perhaps. But the tension between the archaeological chapters of Thucydides and the main body of his narrative on the Peloponnesian war is undeniable, and possibly related (as was suggested a long time ago) to two different literary projects.[36]

B. In this reading of the *Rhetoric*, it seems likely that the archaeological (that is, antiquarian) dimension of Thucydides' work might have found a sympathetic reader in Aristotle, whose general attitude toward history could be reconsidered in the light of the references to an inferential knowledge of the past included in this writing. Finley's blunt dismissal of *Poetics* 1459b on history should be qualified by his own later remark on the importance attached to archival research by the followers of Aristotle. A few years ago, Gregory Nagy, in a remarkable essay, emphasized the juridical dimension of Greek historiography by comparing it to public arbitration.[37] Nagy's conclusions seem to converge with the reading of Aristotle's *Rhetoric* being proposed here.

C. What has been said about the discontinuities concealed in our intellectual vocabulary can be applied to "rhetoric" as well. We have tried to demonstrate that Aristotle's *rētorikē technē* was deeply different from the uses of rhetoric today. In the next chapter we shall examine this momentous historical gap and its implications. But here and now, a clarification of the contemporary debate on the relationship between rhetoric and history is in order.

VIII

Once again we should turn to the work of that outstanding scholar, Arnaldo Momigliano. In his essay "The Rhetoric of History and the History of Rhetoric," published in 1981, he strongly objected to the attempt made by Hayden White, Peter Munz, and others to regard "historians, like any other narrators, as rhetoricians to be characterized by their modes of speech." "I fear the consequences of his approach to historiography," Momigliano wrote, "because he [White] has eliminated the research for truth as the main task of the historian."[38] What has transpired since then on the intellectual scene at large proves that Momigliano's fears were well founded. The debate about truth is one of the most important (in a sense, *the* most important) intellectual issues with which we are confronted; Momigliano's standpoint is convincing, and he proved his case very effectively. But the general framework of his argument is not so persuasive. Having spoken with irony of "the fascination that the rediscovery of rhetoric is exercising on the students of history of historiography at present," Momigliano remarked that in a historical perspective "a self-conscious interference of rhetoricians with the field of historiography is perhaps not earlier than Isocrates in the fourth century B.C."[39] Here and elsewhere Momigliano did not mention Aristotle's *Rhetoric*. Another passage from the same essay will clarify the reasons for this curiously missing reference:

[A]ny question any historian asks about something which happened implies the possibility that what he thinks happened did not happen: therefore the historian not only has to make sense of the event but also has to make sure that it was an event. Unlike Munz, I am not disgusted by the comparison this suggests with the daily work of a policeman (or of a judge). Both have to make sense of certain events after having ascertained that the events happened. But their activities are confined to a few categories of events within defined chronological limits and seldom have any interest for the outsider. Historians are paid by society to inquire about events of general interest, the reality and the meaning of which cannot be established without complex knowledge. Policemen are not supposed to understand, still less to publish, medieval charters. Even judges nowadays seldom have to deal with them: when they do, they are welcome to the historians' table.[40]

Judges and historians share a concern for ascertaining facts, which may include rumors affecting financial markets, myths, legends, and so forth; therefore, they share a concern for proof.[41] These convergences should not prevent us from seeing that judges and historians are separated by two fundamental divergences. Judges are supposed to pronounce sentences, historians are not; judges are concerned *only* with events leading to individual responsibilities, historians are not. Nevertheless, Momigliano's suggestion that while judges are interested in events that "seldom have any interest for the outsider," "historians are paid by society to inquire about events of general interest" does not seem acceptable. More and more often in the last decades historians have been working with such judiciary sources as Inquisition trials, court records, and so forth, which deal with the lives of obscure people and unimportant events. The way in which these supposedly uninteresting facts can sometimes be transformed into "events of general interest" does not concern us here. But it should be pointed out that what led many historians to work with judiciary sources also brought to the fore, first, the ambiguous contiguities between judges and historians and, second, the relevance of judicial rhetoric to any discussion on the methodology of history. Surprisingly, neither the authors of recent controversial books on the *Shoah*—largely based on court records of postwar trials—nor their critics, paid much attention to these methodological issues.[42]

The fashionable reduction of history to rhetoric cannot be rejected by claiming that the relationship between history and rhetoric has always been tenuous and marginal. In my view, that reduction can and must be rejected by rediscovering the intellectual richness of the tradition started by Aristotle, particularly its central argument: that proofs, far from being incompatible with rhetoric, are its fundamental core.

Notes

1. I followed (with changes) W. Hamilton Fyfe's translation in The Loeb Classical Library.

2. M. I. Finley, "Myth, Memory and History" (1965), in *The Use and Abuse of History* (London, 1975), p. 11. This remark is indirectly recalled in Finley's last book, *Ancient History: Evidence and Models* (London, 1985), p. 118, n. 30.

3. See my introduction, as well as my essay, "Just One Witness," in

Probing the Limits of Representation: Nazism and the "Final Solution," ed. S. Friedlander (Cambridge, Mass., 1992), pp. 82–96, 350–55.

4. Aristotle, *The "Art" of Rhetoric,* The Loeb Classical Library, tr. G. H. Freese. F. Solmsen, *Die Entwicklung der aristotelischen Logik und Rhetorik,* Neue Philologische Untersuchungen, 4 (Berlin, 1929), pp. 227–28, suggests that Aristotle made a "synthesis" between the two points of view.

5. The necessity of comparing "the attitude of Aristotle toward history . . . with the attitude of Aristotle toward rhetoric" has been recognized and immediately set aside by S. Mazzarino (*Il pensiero storico classico* [Bari, 1983], 1:415) who, significantly enough, ignores the issue of proof.

6. See R. Thomas, *Oral Tradition and Written Record in Classical Athens,* 2nd ed. (Cambridge, England, 1990).

7. On "syllogism" as a misleading translation of *syllogismos,* see J. Barnes, "Proof and the Syllogism," in *Aristotle on Science: the "Posterior Analytics," Proceedings of the Eighth Symposium Aristotelicum . . . ,* ed. E. Berti (Padua, 1981), pp. 17ff., especially p. 23, n. 7.

8. M. F. Burnyeat, "Enthymeme: Aristotle on the Logic of Persuasion," in *Aristotle's Rhetoric: Philosophical Studies,* ed. D. J. Furley and A. Nehamas (Princeton, 1994), pp. 3–55. I should like to thank Julia Annas for this reference.

9. Burnyeat, "Enthymeme," pp. 22–23.

10. Ibid. p. 5.

11. Herodotus, *Histories,* 4 The Loeb Classical Library, tr. A. D. Godley (Cambridge, Mass., and London, 1946).

12. Lucian of Samosata, *Anacharsis (Dialogues,* The Loeb Classical Library, vol. 4, ed. A. M. Harmon (Cambridge, Mass., and London, 1925). See G. C. Roscioni, *Sulle tracce dell' "Esploratore turco"* (Milan, 1992), p. 164, as well as my paper "Anacharsis interroga gli indigeni. Una nuova lettura di un vecchio best-seller," in *L'Histoire grande ouverte: Hommages à Emmanuel Le Roy Ladurie,* ed. A. Burguière, J. Goy, and M.-J. Tits-Dieuaide (Paris, 1997), pp. 337–46.

13. E. E. Ryan, *Aristotle's Theory of Rhetorical Argumentation* (Montreal, 1984), pp. 42–43.

14. L. Moretti, "Olympionikai, i vincitori negli antichi agoni olimpici," *Atti dell'Accademia nazionale dei Lincei: Memorie della classe di scienze morali, storiche e filologiche,* ser. 8, vol. 8 (1957), fasc. 2, p. 105, n. 33, with bibliography.

15. A. Körte, "Die Entstehung der Olympionikenliste," *Hermes* 39 (1904): 224–43.

16. R. Weil, *Aristote et l'histoire* (Paris, 1960), pp. 131–37.

17. Plato, *Hippias Major,* The Loeb Classical Library, tr. H. N. Fowler.

18. A. Momigliano, "Ancient History and the Antiquarian" (1950), in *Contributo alla storia degli studi classici* (Rome, 1955), p. 70 and n. 5.

19. A. Momigliano, "Ideali di vita nella sofistica: Ippia e Crizia" (1930), in *Quarto contributo alla storia degli studi classici e del mondo antico* (Rome, 1969), pp. 145–54, especially p. 149.

20. I. Düring, *Aristotele,* Italian trans. (Milan, 1976), pp. 64–65.

21. G. E. M. de Ste. Croix, "Aristotle on History and Poetry (*Poetics* 9.1451a36–b11)," in *The Ancient Historian and His Materials: Essays in Honour of C. E. Stevens on His Seventieth Birthday*, ed. B. Levick (Westmead, Farnborough, 1975), pp. 45–58. See also D. M. Pippidi, "Aristote et Thucydide. En marge du chapitre IX de la *Poétique*," in *Mélanges de philologie, de littérature et d'histoire anciennes, offerts à J. Marouzeau . . .*, (Paris, 1948), pp. 483–90.

22. *Index Thucydideus, ex Bekkeri editione sterotypa confectus a M. H. N. von Essen Dre Hamburgensi* (Darmstadt, 1964).

23. See E. Täubler's path-breaking book, *Die Archaeologie des Thukydides* (Leipzig and Berlin, 1927; reprint 1979). By the same author, see also *Ausgewählte Schriften zur Alten Geschichte* (Stuttgart, 1987), with an introduction by G. Alföldy (including a list of obituaries and reviews) and a bibliography. From a similar perspective, see J. Gommel (*Rhetorisches Argumentum bei Thukydides, Spudasmata, vol. 10* [Hildesheim, 1966]), who insists above all on the connection between Thucydides and Antiphon the rhetor.

24. M. F. Burnyeat noticed that the distinction had no basis in earlier rhetoric: "The origins of non-deductive inference," in J. Barnes et al., *Science and Speculation*, Proceedings of the Second Symposium Hellenisticum (Cambridge, England, 1982), pp. 193–238, especially p. 196, n. 10. See also the commentary to the first book of Aristotle's *Rhetoric* by W. M. A. Grimaldi, S.J. (New York, 1980), pp. 63ff.

25. M. Finley, *Ancient History: Evidence and Methods*, pp. 28, 53, 172, n. 22.

26. Thucydides, as F. Hartog remarks in the new introduction to his *Le miroir d'Hérodote* (Paris, 1991), pp. iii, xv, never uses the word *historia*.

27. On Thucydides' use of enthymemes, see J. de Romilly, *La construction de la vérité chez Thucydide* (Paris, 1990), pp. 73ff. On p. 76 she remarks: "si la place des réflexions correspond à une habitude rhétorique, leur fonction n'est en aucune façon purement rhétorique: . . . elles font . . . partie de l'argumentation"—which is, of course, consistent with the ancient notion of rhetoric.

28. A. Momigliano, "Storiografia su tradizione scritta e storiografia su tradizione orale" (1961–62), *Terzo contributo alla storia degli studi classici e del mondo antico* (Rome, 1966), I:13–22 (on p. 16 the allusion to Xenophanes).

29. *I presocratici*, ed. A. Lami (Milan, 1991), pp. 178ff. (Hyppolitus).

30. *Oedipus Tyrannus*, 109. See B. Williams, *Shame and Necessity* (Berkeley, 1993), pp. 58–59. I am grateful to Luciano Canfora who, in a now remote debate, urged me to study the meaning of *sēmeion* in Thucydides (*Quaderni di storia* 12 [July–Dec. 1980]: pp. 49–50, for my essay "Clues: Roots of an Evidential Paradigm," in *Clues, Myths, and the Historical Method* [Baltimore, 1989], pp. 96–125). See also F. Hartog, "L'oeil de Thucydide et l'histoire 'véritable,'" *Poétique* 49 (Feb. 1982), pp. 21–30, and, more generally, Burnyeat, "The Origins of Non-Deductive Inference." See now J. Hankinson, "*Sēmeion e tekmērion*. L'evoluzione del

vocabolario di segni e indicazioni nella Grecia classica," *I Greci*, ed. S. Settis, vol. 2, tome 2 (Turin, 1997), pp. 1169–87.

31. H. D. Westlake, "*Hōs eikos* in Thucydides," *Hermes* 86 (1958): 447–52; P. Butti de Lima, *L'inchiesta e la prova: Immagine storiografica, pratica giuridica e retorica nella Grecia classica* (Turin, 1996), pp. 160ff.

32. On this matter, see my *Il giudice e lo storico: Considerazioni in margine al processo Sofri* (Turin, 1991), p. 117, n. 72.

33. Mazzarino, *Il pensiero storico* I:410. See, instead, Finley, *The Use and Abuse of History*, p. 11.

34. Burnyeat, "Enthymeme," p. 38.

35 See A. Momigliano, "Ancient History and the Antiquarian" (1950), in *Contributo alla storia degli studi classici*, pp. 67–106.

36. K. Ziegler, "Der Ursprung der Exkurse im Thukydides," *Rheinisches Museum*, N.F. 78 (1929): 58–67.

37. G. Nagy, "Mythe et prose en Grèce archaïque: l'*aînos*," in *Métamorphose du mythe en Grèce antique*, ed. C. Calame (Geneva, 1988), pp. 229–42.

38. A. Momigliano, "The Rhetoric of History and the History of Rhetoric: On Hayden White's Tropes" (1981), in *Settimo contributo alla storia degli studi classici e del mondo antico* (Rome, 1984), pp. 49–59, at p. 49.

39. Momigliano, "The Rhetoric of History," p. 58.

40. Ibid., pp. 57–58.

41. I dealt with these issues in *Il giudice e lo storico*; "Checking the Evidence: the Judge and the Historian," *Critical Inquiry* 18, no. 1 (1991): 79–92.

42. C. R. Browning, *Ordinary Men: Reserve Police Battalion 101 and the Final Solution in Poland* (New York, 1992). On a much less sophisticated level, see also D. J. Goldhagen, *Hitler's Willing Executioners. Ordinary Germans and the Holocaust* (New York, 1996).

2 Lorenzo Valla on the "Donation of Constantine"

The oration on the *Donation of Constantine* was written by Lorenzo Valla, the Italian humanist, in 1440, in his youth (he was born in Piacenza, c. 1407), under circumstances that seem clear: Valla's patron, Alphonse of Aragon, was fighting a war against the pope, Eugene IV, who had tried to undermine his accession to the throne of Naples. By exposing a well-known piece of papal propaganda as a forgery, Valla created a most effective piece of antipapal propaganda.

But why are we still reading it, after five hundred years? The target of Valla's oration was the so-called *constitutum Constantini*, a document that had circulated widely throughout Europe during the Middle Ages. According to this text, the Roman Emperor Constantine, having been miraculously healed from leprosy by Pope Sylvester, converted to Christianity and bestowed a third of the Empire on the Roman Church as a sign of gratitude. Today scholars believe that the *constitutum* was probably forged in the mid-eighth century by a papal notary, in order to provide a pseudo-legal basis for papal pretensions to temporal power. But for a long time the story of the donation of Constantine, which seems so utterly unbelievable to us, did not raise any doubt whatsoever. Its truthfulness was taken for granted even by Dante, among innumerable others. In a famous passage of his *Commedia* he complained, addressing himself to pope Boniface VIII, that the donation of Constantine had unfortunately created the premises for the corruption of the Roman Church:

> Ahi, Constantin, di quanto mal fu matre,
> non la tua conversion, ma quella dote
> che da te prese il primo ricco patre!"
> *(Inferno* XV, 115–17)

(Alas, Constantine, what a great evil was generated, not by your conversion but by the endowment which for the first time transformed the pope into a rich man!)

Medieval legal writers, such as John of Paris, rejected the legitimacy of the donation since the emperor, as the "administrator of the Empire," could not dispose of it through a private act.[1]

In the mid-fifteenth century, when Valla wrote his oration, the authenticity of the *constitutum Constantini* had already been challenged. Nicholas of Cusa, the great philosopher and a cardinal of the Roman Church, was among those who openly rejected it. In fact, the scandal provoked by Valla's text was related not so much to its content as to the unprecedented violence of its language. Valla's aggressive tone in addressing the pope explains why the oration did not appear in print until 1506. In 1518 Ulrich von Hutten, the German humanist, republished it as a political manifesto denouncing the ambitions and greed of the Roman Church.[2]

In the seventeenth and eighteenth centuries, Valla's image changed: more and more often he came to be regarded by philologists and antiquarians as a forerunner of the developing critical approach to historical evidence.[3] In the nineteenth century scholars usually emphasized the political circumstances in which Valla had written his oration. These divergent (although not necessarily incompatible) readings are quite typical of the effort to interpret what we call a classic. But a survey of the different ways in which a text has been viewed through the centuries cannot replace our own interpretation. What does Valla's oration on the donation of Constantine mean for us today?

We must start by looking at how Valla himself read his own text. This will be, however, only the beginning. Valla's self-perception cannot be identical to our own. In Immanuel Kant's famous words, we can (at least in principle) understand Plato better than did Plato himself. Valla's self-perception and our perspective of his work cannot coincide.[4]

II

Valla commented on his own oration when he sent it to two fellow humanists, Giovanni Tortelli and Giovanni Aurispa. On May 25, 1440, Valla wrote to Tortelli, a close friend to whom he used to submit his own writings: "this is a piece about canon law and theology, attacking all canon law experts and theologians" (*rem canonici iuris et theologie, sed contra omnes canonistas atque omnes theologos*). On December 31, 1443 in a letter addressed to Aurispa, Valla remarked that he had never written "a piece as rhetorical as this one" (*orationem meam . . . qua nihil magis oratorium scripsi*)."[5]

The two opinions were not contradictory: the former focused on the content, the latter on the formal features of the text. Valla is saying that he dealt with topics related to canon law and theology in a polemical way, relying upon the instruments of rhetoric.[6] But the latter part of this remark confronts us with a problem. Valla's oration is roughly divided into two parts. In the first, Constantine's alleged donation of a large part of the imperial domains to Pope Sylvester is rejected on the grounds of its psychological implausibility. Here we have a series of purely fictitious dialogues between Constantine and his children, and Constantine and the pope. In the second, the *constitutum Costantini*, the document on which the alleged donation is based, is rejected as a forgery. A detailed discussion focuses on the anachronisms, inconsistencies, and misunderstandings of the piece. The two following passages will give some idea of the wide difference between the arguments used by Valla in the two sections.

If Constantine had donated his empire to God, Valla contends,

he would offend his sons (which was not the case with Jeroboam), humiliate his friends, ignore his relatives, injure his country, plunge everybody into grief, and forget his own interests!

But if, having been such a man as he was, he had been transformed as it were into another man, there would certainly not have been lacking those who would warn him, most of all his sons, his relatives, and his friends. Who does not think that they would have gone at once to the emperor? Picture them to yourself, when the purpose of Constantine had become known, trembling, hastening to fall with groans and tears at the feet of the prince, and saying:

"Is it thus that you, a father hitherto most affectionate toward your sons, despoil your sons, disinherit them, disown them?

and so on and so forth.

Now for a quotation from the second part of the oration: a comment on a passage from the *constitutum Costantini* in which the emperor asserts that, "together with all the satraps and the whole senate, as well as with the elite and the whole population subject to the Roman Church" (*cum omnibus satrapis nostris et universo senatu, optimatibus etiam et cum cuncto populo imperio Romane ecclesie subiacenti*), he gave to the popes a power that was much larger than his own. "You villain, you rascal!" Valla exclaims, addressing himself to the unknown forger of the *constitutum Constantini*.

O thou scoundrel, thou villain! The same history [the Life of Sylvester] which you allege as your evidence, says that for a long time none of senatorial rank was willing to accept the Christian religion, and that Constantine solicited the poor with bribes to be baptized. And you say that within the first days, immediately, the Senate, the nobles, the satraps, as though already Christians, with the Caesar passed decrees for the honoring of the Roman church! What! How do you want to have satraps come in here? Numskull, blockhead! Do the Caesars speak thus; are Roman decrees usually drafted thus? Whoever heard of satraps being mentioned in the councils of the Romans? I do not remember ever to have read of any Roman satrap being mentioned, or even of a satrap in any of the Roman provinces. (Tr. Coleman)

The gap between Valla the rhetorician and polemist, on the one hand, and Valla the forerunner of modern historical method, on the other, seems rather wide. This difficulty is part of a larger problem. In the last twenty-five years the notion of proof has often been regarded as a typical trait, or even a symbol, of positivist historiography. Rhetoric has been opposed to proof, and the emphasis on the rhetorical dimension of history, not to mention the identification of the former with the latter, has become, as I stated in the first chapter, the most effective weapon in a battle against the positivism that is still so prominent in the historical profession. The so-called linguistic trend should be labelled, in fact, a turn toward rhetoric.

III

The origins of this dramatic intellectual change can be found in the work of Friedrich Nietzsche. But the use of rhetorical tools in a skeptical perspective was not a complete novelty. In a sense, Nietzsche, professor of philology at the University of Basel, was following, two thousand years later, in the footsteps of the sophists. This intellectual heritage is explicitly acknowledged in the first page of Nancy Struever's *The Language of History in the Renaissance: Rhetoric and Historical Consciousness in Florentine Humanism* (Princeton, 1970). Struever did not hesitate to admit having been inspired by "a recent change in fashion" in her analysis of the attitudes of Leonardo Bruni, Poggio Bracciolini, and, in a much more marginal way, Lorenzo Valla, toward history and language.

The "recent change in fashion" mentioned by Struever can be dated with some precision. It was detected at its very beginning, and then effectively promoted, by Roland Barthes, that ultrasensitive barometer of contemporary intellectual life. In an essay published in 1967 in the *Times Literary Supplement*, Barthes contrasted structuralism as rhetoric to structuralism as science, the latter being close to what he called the "bourgeois positivism" of *sciences humaines*. In the same year Barthes published "Le discours de l'histoire," the well-known and influential essay that viewed historiography as a form of rhetoric.[7] Notwithstanding Barthes's tactical move to reinterpret structuralism *sub specie rhetorica* instead of rejecting it altogether, these two texts already pointed to poststructuralism or postmodernism: the intellectual climate in which we still live. Whatever our attitude toward it, there is no doubt that the "recent change in fashion" adduced by Struever must be taken very seriously. Thirty years later we have to admit that rhetoric's return to the intellectual scene was not an ephemeral event.

But did we really need Barthes (or Nietzsche) to discover the part played by rhetoric in the historical works of Leonardo Bruni, Lorenzo Valla, or Poggio Bracciolini? Hardly. As is well known, Paul Oskar Kristeller, the leading authority on Italian humanism, based his highly influential interpretation of this historical movement precisely on the rediscovery of the role of rhetoric within it. We are therefore confronted with an ambiguity, one that needs to be deciphered. But first, a short digression: a footnote to the history (or prehistory) of Kristeller's interpretation.

IV

The earliest version of Kristeller's global approach to Italian humanism can be found in his "Humanism and Scholasticism in the Italian Renaissance," an essay published in 1944–45.[8] According to the author, the dominant feature of Italian humanism was neither a fuller knowledge of classical antiquity, nor a new philosophy attacking the Scholastic tradition. The most important element was the link between the humanists and the European rhetorical tradition. In Kristeller's presentation, "rhetoric" had lost the derogatory connotations that long had been attached to it, especially in the writings of those who decried Italian humanism as an empty, wordy, superficial intellectual movement, devoted to rhetoric in the worst sense of the word.

This positive evaluation had already been suggested some years earlier by Delio Cantimori, the historian of Italian sixteenth-century "heretics," in his essay "Rhetoric and Politics in Italian Humanism," published in the *Journal of the Warburg Institute* in 1937. Cantimori explored the political implications of humanistic rhetoric through a specific case study: the debates that took place in the Orti Oricellari, the gardens of the Rucellai family, in Florence. Besides oratorical and literary taste, "rhetoric" meant, according to Cantimori, "a crude, naive, rather inarticulate, but genuine faith . . . in a word, an ideology."[9]

Here it will be useful to add a few words concerning Cantimori's complex political biography. As a young man, he had been first a follower of the tradition that went back to Giuseppe Mazzini; then he became a left-wing fascist and a protégé of the philosopher and minister of education Giovanni Gentile; in the mid-thirties he established a link with underground groups of the Italian communist party (he became a member in 1948 and left in 1956). Significantly, in the same years in which he discovered the importance of humanistic rhetoric as a form of political "ideology," Cantimori was paying close attention to the phenomenon of propaganda in twentieth-century mass societies.[10]

Kristeller, who left Germany in 1933, spent a few years in Italy under the protection of Gentile, who found him a position as instructor at the Scuola Normale in Pisa. Cantimori was teaching history in the same institution during this time. When Kristeller was compelled to leave Italy in 1938, as a consequence of the Fascist anti-Semitic laws, Cantimori wrote letters of recommendation for him to F. C. Church, the American historian of Italian heretics, and to R. H. Bainton. In Kristeller's approach to humanism there is no trace of Cantimori's emphasis on the political implications of humanistic rhetoric.[11] Nevertheless, the discussions that took place in Pisa in the thirties between these two great scholars were undoubtedly significant for both.

Nearly forty years after his "Humanism and Scholasticism in the Italian Renaissance," Kristeller insisted that he had never regarded rhetoric as the crucial aspect of Italian humanism, as some scholars, including Nancy Struever, argued that it was.[12] But this misunderstanding had deeper roots: the point was the meaning of rhetoric, not the degree of emphasis placed on it. When she wrote that "rhetoric is in many ways hostile to the modern notion of philology," Struever was clearly advocating an antipositivist interpretation of Italian humanism. Kristeller rejected this argument, which was explicitly based on the work of his former teacher, Martin Heidegger (as well as, of course, on Nietzsche's).[13]

V

As we have seen, Valla included in his work on the donation of Constantine rhetoric and philology, fictitious dialogues and detailed analyses of documentary proofs. The aforementioned remark by Struever, so clearly indebted to a specific and still current intellectual attitude, seems quite incompatible with Valla's text. It would become somewhat more acceptable if it were reformulated as: "the *modern* notion of rhetoric is in many ways hostile to philology." But what did Valla mean by rhetoric?

Hanna H. Gray remarked that Valla defined his oration on the donation of Constantine as a *declamatio*, a word used by Quintilian as a label for a rhetorical exercise based on the alternating demonstration of opposite arguments, which included the authenticity or falsehood of specific texts.[14] If this argument could be accepted, Struever would be absolutely right: her own interpretation of rhetoric in a skeptical perspective would coincide with Valla's. But Valla never dreamed of arguing both the falsehood and the authenticity of the donation of Constantine. Moreover, as W. Setz has remarked, the word *declamatio* was used not by Valla, but either by later scribes or by editors such as Ulrich von Hutten.[15]

But Gray was absolutely right to mention Quintilian in this context. In the fifth book of Quintilian's *Institutio Oratoria*, Valla would have found a long discussion on proofs ("De probationum divisione"). Among proofs that he called *inartificiales*, that is, not based on the art of rhetoric, Quintilian listed "prejudices, rumours, tortures, documents [*tabulae*], oaths and witnesses, which provide the basic evidence in court debates." In the annotated edition of Quintilian's *Institutio Oratoria*, published in Venice in 1493, we read that *tabulae* meant "wills and charters" (*instrumenta*). The *constitutum Constantini* fitted very well in the latter category. The comment to the 1493 Quintilian edition, signed by Raffaele Regio, was in fact based, without any acknowledgment, upon the notes on the *Institutio Oratoria* that were part of Valla's *Nachlaß*. One year later, this literary theft triggered the publication of a new edition of Quintilian in Venice, which at last displayed the name of Valla on the front page, and included some of his notes.[16]

Valla owned two manuscripts of the *Institutio Oratoria*. One of them has disappeared. The one that survives, *Parisinus latinus* 7723, has a subscription in Valla's hand, dated 9 December 1444. We know for certain that Valla's commentary on Quintilian's text, which certainly continued after this date, had already begun in August 1441, as we learn from a letter to Giovanni Tortelli.[17] It is possible to conclude that Valla wrote the *Donation of Constantine* after he had started working on his notes on Quintilian. A detailed analysis of the possible interactions between these works would require a critical edition of *Parisinus latinus* 7723 (which so far does not exist), but there are some obvious convergences. The demonstration that the *constitutum Constantini* is a forgery closely follows Quintilian's suggestions: the document lacks verisimilitude; it is refuted by other documents; it includes chronological data that are intrinsically contradictory such as the mention of Constantinople, incompatible with a document that was supposed to have been written immediately after Constantine's conversion. Valla presumably put the *constitutum Constantini* in the category of blatantly false documents—a very large category, according to Quintilian.[18]

Valla was so fervently fond of Quintilian that (as we learn from a letter of his to Giovanni Tortelli) he valued him above Demosthenes, above Cicero, even above Homer.[19] But Quintilian, who was certainly a very effective writer and presumably an excellent teacher, cannot be regarded as an original thinker. "Prejudices, rumors, tortures, documents [*tabulae*], oaths and witnesses": the source of this quotation from Quintilian's *Institutio Oratoria* was simply Aristotle's *Rhetoric*. *Tabulae*, for instance, was a Latin equivalent for the Greek *syngraphai*.[20] The distinction between "artificial" (*entechnoi*) and "inartificial" (*atechnoi*) proofs, made by Quintilian at the beginning (5.1.1) of the fifth book of the *Institutio Oratoria*, was also explicitly based on Aristotle, although Quintilian remarked that at that point everybody agreed on it. In fact, although it has been suggested that Quintilian possibly never had direct access to the whole of the *Rhetoric*, his approach was quite close to Aristotle's.[21]

VI

The existence of an intellectual tradition passing from Aristotle to Quintilian, from Quintilian to Valla fits perfectly with the reading of Aristotle's *Rhetoric*. Aristotle's approach, focusing on proof as the rational core of rhetoric, utterly contradicts the current self-referential image of rhetoric, based on the assumption that rhetoric and proof are basically incompatible. How has it been possible to suppress so deeply the central argument of one of the fundamental texts of our intellectual tradition?[22] How has it been possible to take for granted the thoroughly naive idea that proof is a positivistic naiveté?

These are, of course, rhetorical questions; complaints disguised as questions to which there are no good answers. But in this context, we might remember that, according to Friedrich Solmsen, a leading authority on the history of ancient rhetoric, the Aristotelian tradition was preserved above all by Cicero. In particular, Solmsen points to Cicero's approach to emotions, which would imply a direct dependence on Aristotle.[23] The evidence for this, an allusion to Aristotle's writings on rhetoric in the dialogue *De oratore* (2.38.160) notwithstanding, is open to discussion. It has been suggested that Cicero's knowledge of Aristotle's *Rhetoric* was based in fact upon a Hellenistic compendium.[24] In any case, Cicero emphasizes both that Aristotle was not a professional orator and that he "despised" the art of rhetoric. Both remarks seem to imply a rather lukewarm attitude: an impression indirectly reinforced by Cicero's remarks about Diogenes, the Stoic philosopher. As an orator Diogenes had a "meagre, dry, compressed" style. On the contrary, Cicero writes, "our rhetoric must be adapted to the ears of the multitude: it must seduce their souls, it must convince their wills, it must demonstrate its arguments by using not the goldsmith's precision balance but a sort of popular scale [*quae non aurificis statera, sed populari quadam trutina examinantur*]." Needless to say, this "popular scale" was as remote as possible from Aristotle's subtle reflections on proofs. The rational core centered on enthymemes, which according to Aristotle was the most important part of rhetoric, did not have any place in this perspective. Cicero's immense authority succeeded in spreading a different, even opposite, image of rhetoric, as a technique based first of all on emotions and only marginally on the scrutiny of proofs.[25] This is indirectly confirmed by the famous definition of history as *opus unum hoc oratorium maxime*, "the only [intellectual] activity which is mostly rhetorical" given by Cicero in his treatise *On Laws* (1.1.5). For centuries these words seemed to confirm the idea that historians and antiquarians were separated by a wide margin.

The attempt to bridge this gap could come only from such a person as Lorenzo Valla, who was totally foreign, and even hostile, to the cult of Cicero. Notwithstanding Solmsen's conclusions, it was undoubtedly Quintilian, not Cicero, who preserved, and in the end transmitted, Aristotle's intellectual legacy concerning rhetoric. Through the *Institutio Oratoria* of his beloved Quintilian, Valla rediscovered the basic core of Aristotle's *Rhetoric*. In this find there was an element of real paradox. Valla never missed an opportunity to express his hostility toward Aristotle as a philosopher. More specifically, in his introduction to the *Gesta Ferdinandi regis Aragonum*, which he wrote in 1445 and 1446, Valla concealed an attack against Aristotle's ideas about history. History, Valla says, is more ancient and therefore more venerable than poetry or philosophy. Annals emerged before poems: Moses and the evangelists were historians. History deals with universals, including poetry and more. The polemical allusion to Aristotle's *Poetics* was clear enough.[26]

In fact, through a few passing remarks Valla rather cryptically suggested a different vision of the historian's work. Writing history is difficult, he said, as we can see from the divergences among eyewitnesses speaking of a given event. In order to ascertain the truth, the historian needs as much accuracy and insight as any judge or physician—a particularly intriguing double analogy.[27] It is hard to see any contradiction between this emphasis on the factual, antiquarian side of history and the statement, also made by Valla in the introduction to his *Gesta Ferdinandi*, that rhetoric is "the mother of history."[28] Aristotle's *Rhetoric*, mediated by Quintilian, gave Valla the opportunity to escape from the limitations of Ciceronian rhetoric. It is not by chance that in 1448 Valla started his translation of Thucydides, a historian whom Cicero had despised for his obscurity, pointing to him as a negative model for orators to avoid (*Orator*, 9.30–32).

VII

Quintilian suggested that chronological data that are intrinsically contradictory can prove that a document is a forgery. But he did not include language. Valla, on the contrary, regarded a word like *satrapis* as proof that the alleged date of the *constitutum Constantini* was untenable. The use of anachronisms as an instrument of historical analysis was a real turning point, which had an enormous long-term impact. Valla's approach led to Mabillon, Montfaucon, and the seventeenth-century erudites of the Congregation of St. Maur, which Marc Bloch regarded as the initiators of the historian's craft in the modern sense of the word. But when Mabillon, in his great work *De re diplomatica libri VI, in quibus quidquid ad veterum instrumentorum antiquitatem, . . . pertinet, explicatur et illustratur* (1681) assumed that the *constitutum Constantini* was a forgery, he did not dare to use the name of Lorenzo Valla.[29]

But what was the source of Valla's approach to language? The answer is rather surprising. Valla's sensitivity to linguistic anachronisms stemmed from the humanistic yearning to revive classical

Latin as a purified language, free of barbarisms. The attempt to resurrect a lost language, which in a sense had never existed, created the conditions for seeing Latin as a language that had undergone different historical stages.[30] When Leonardo Bruni and Flavio Biondo engaged in 1435 in their memorable debate over the language (or languages) spoken by ancient Romans, both parties implicitly agreed that Latin should be considered as a historical entity.[31] Leonardo Bruni's *De interpretatione recta*, a defense of his Latin translation of Aristotle's *Nicomachean Ethics*, which exposed the Greek and vernacular echoes marring an earlier translation, opened the way for Valla to use such traces as evidence for the forgery of the *constitutum Constantini*.[32] Bruni compared the ignorant translators who distorted Aristotle's originals to someone who might have disfigured a painting by Apelles or other famous Greek painters.[33] The genuine translator, ready to identify himself with the author's mind and intelligence, was close—Bruni said—to a copyist who would try to imitate the features of an original painting.[34] About the year 1420, when Bruni wrote these words, all Florentine workshops were busily producing replicas.[35] A few decades later, faking gems and *sculture all'antica*, as well as deliberate forgeries of ancient objects, had become a widespread practice.[36] The attempts made by humanists, antiquarians, translators into the vernacular, copyists, and forgers either to reconstitute or to recreate the history of what had gone before, also implied a critical distance from it.[37]

IX

This attitude toward the past is the background of Valla's *Oratio in principio studii*, the inaugural lecture he read at the University of Rome on 18 October 1455.[38] The size of the Roman Empire, Valla noticed, contributed to the spread of all sorts of human endeavors, through emulation and competition. A sculptor or a painter might never try to achieve perfection in his own art if he worked alone. Quintilian had compared words to coins: Valla compared the Latin tongue to currency as an instrument that allowed all sorts of intellectual and commercial exchanges.[39] Just as the invention of money encouraged the circulation of products, so the existence of a common tongue—Latin—helped develop intellectual life in the provinces of the Roman empire: Cicero was from Arpino, Vergil from Mantua, Seneca from Cordova, Livy from Padua, Priscianus from Caesarea, Ulpianus (the great Roman jurist) from Phoenicia. After the collapse of the Roman empire, Asia and Africa, which had belonged to it, fell back into their previous barbarous condition. In Europe, Valla continued, the Roman Church protected the Latin tongue by using it both as a sacred and as an administrative language. Under the patronage of the popes, letters and the arts were flourishing again.

This is, if not the first, one of the earliest occurrences of the word "Europe" used in a cultural, rather than a merely geographical sense.[40] Europe, as heir of the Roman Empire, emerged from Valla's words as a distinct civilization based on competition and commerce, and unified by a single language (vernaculars were simply ignored). The praise of the Roman Church for having preserved the Latin tongue seems an obvious flattery. Less obvious, and seemingly unnoticed, was the implicit model for Valla's boldly compressed historical sketch: Eusebius of Caesarea's *Ecclesiastical History*, a work Valla had widely used in his opuscule against the *Donation of Constantine*. After having mentioned the (legendary) praise of Christian religion pronounced by the emperor Tiberius, Eusebius had written: "For heavenly providence had designed putting this in his mind in order that the word [*logos*] of the gospel might have an unimpeded beginning, and traverse the earth in all directions" (2.2.4). For both Eusebius and Valla the Roman empire played a providential role. But in the latter's account *logos* (*sermo*, as Erasmus will translate John 1:1)[41] turned into *lingua Latina*, the Latin tongue; the diffusion of Christianity into the diffusion of commerce and arts.

Valla's inaugural lecture rings out today as a prophecy of the European expansion overseas that was about to begin. At this point, it may be useful to turn our attention, through a specific case study, to the role played in that movement by expectations related to Latin civilization and rhetoric.

Notes

1. E. H. Kantorowicz, *The King's Two Bodies* (Princeton, 1957), p. 190, n. 310.

2. Valla's text has been critically edited by W. Setz, *Lorenzo Vallas Schrift gegen die Konstantinische Schenkung: De falso credita et emen- tita Constantini donatione. Zur Interpretation und Wirkungsgeschichte.* Bibliothek des Deutschen Historischen Instituts in Rom, vol. 44 (Tübingen, 1975); see also the review by R. Fubini in *Studi medievali* 3, no. 20 (1979): 221–28. The rejection by Cusanus of the *constitutum* was familiar to Valla, as has been convincingly argued by R. Fubini, "Contes- tazioni quattrocentesche della donazione di Costantino: Niccolò Cusano, Lorenzo Valla," in *Costantino il Grande dall'antichità all'umanesimo,* ed. G. Bonamente and F. Fusco (Macerata, 1992), 1:385–431, especially pp. 403 ff.

3. See the entry "Valla, Laurent" in Bayle's *Dictionnaire historique et critique* (Rotterdam, 1702), 3:2934–37, as well as the allusions to Valla's remarks on Livy in the entry "Tanaquil" (*ibid.*, p. 2833). The relevance of the latter has been stressed by A. Momigliano, *Sui fondamenti della storia antica* (Turin, 1984), p. 276, n. 13.

4. On Kant's famous remark, that we can (at least in principle) under- stand Plato better than did Plato himself, see P. C. Bori, *L'interpretazione infinita: L'ermeneutica cristiana antica e le sue trasformazioni* (Bologna, 1987), pp. 141–49.

5. See *Laurentii Valle epistole,* ed. O. Besomi and M. Regoliosi (Padua, 1984), pp. 192, 252. Setz (pp. 46ff.) interprets the texts mentioned above differently. (After having written these pages I read V. De Caprio's excel- lent paper "Retorica e ideologia nella *Declamatio* di Lorenzo Valla sulla donazione di Costantino," *Paragone-Letteratura* 29, no. 338 [1978]: 36–56, which deals with Valla's attitude towards Quintilian. De Caprio's conclu- sions are close to mine, although his research followed a different path (see also his *La tradizione e il trauma: Idee del Rinascimento romano* [Vi- terbo, 1991]). Valla's opuscule has been read as an example of Christian rhetoric arguing for a renascence of "pre-Constantinian Christianity" by S. Camporeale ("Lorenzo Valla's *Oratio* on the Pseudo-Donation of Con- stantine: Dissent and Innovation in Early Renaissance Humanism," *Jour- nal of the History of Ideas* [1996]: 9–26, especially p. 25, with references to the author's previous works) and as an example of rejection of rhetoric by R. Fubini ("Contestazioni quattrocentesche," pp. 425ff., particularly p. 428). The notion of rhetoric discussed in this book implies a disagreement with both approaches.

6. "Prope tota in contentione versatur," a basically polemical piece, Valla wrote to Guarino of Verona on 25 October 1443 (*Laurentii Valle epistole,* p. 245).

7. See R. Barthes, "De la science à la littérature," and "Le discours de l'histoire," both republished in *Le bruissement de la langue: Essais cri- tiques IV* (Paris, 1984). The former paper is mentioned by N. Struever, *The Language of History in the Renaissance: Rhetoric and Historical Con- sciousness in Florentine Humanism* (Princeton, 1970), p.15.

8. See P. O. Kristeller, *Studies in Renaissance Thought and Letters* (Rome, 1956), pp. 553–83, as well as "Paul Oskar Kristeller and his Contri-

bution to Scholarship," in *Philosophy and Humanism: Renaissance Essays in Honor of Paul Oskar Kristeller*, ed. E. P. Mahoney (Leiden, 1976), pp. 8–9 ("a crucial and seminal paper").

9. The quotation is taken from the unpublished version, now appearing as an appendix to the new edition of Cantimori's major work, the *Eretici italiani del Cinquecento e altri scritti*, ed. A. Prosperi (Turin, 1992), pp. 485–511, especially p. 490. (Prosperi's introduction is very relevant.) In Frances Yates's shortened translation, the word "ideology" is qualified, and softened, as "aesthetico-moral ideology" ("Rhetoric and Politics in Italian Humanism," *Journal of the Warburg Institute* 1 [1937]: 83–102, especially p. 86).

10. See "Appunti sulla propaganda," first published in *Civiltà fascista*, 1941, now republished in D. Cantimori, *Politica e storia contemporanea: Scritti 1927–1942* (Turin, 1991), pp. 683–99. In the same collection, see (pp. 192–96), the review of Ernesto Codignola, *Il rinnovamento spirituale dei giovani* (Milan, 1934), which stresses the need for a serious analysis of Nazi propaganda, even in its "crude and naive" forms.

11. See D. Cantimori, *Studi di storia* (Turin, 1959), pp. 391–98, especially p. 395; A. Prosperi, introduction to *Eretici italiani del Cinquecento*, p. xiv; P. O. Kristeller and M. L. King, "Iter Kristellerianum: The European Journey (1905–1939)," *Renaissance Quarterly* 47 (1994): 907–29, especially p. 920.

12. See P. O. Kristeller, "Rhetoric in Medieval and Renaissance Culture," in *Renaissance Eloquence*, ed. J. J. Murphy (Berkeley, 1983), pp. 1–19, especially p. 2.

13. On Kristeller's relationship with Heidegger, see the recollections of the former in "Iter Kristellerianum."

14. See H. H. Gray, "Renaissance Humanism: the Pursuit of Eloquence" (1963), reprinted in *Renaissance Essays*, ed. P. O. Kristeller and P. P. Wiener (New York, 1968), pp. 199–216.

15. See Setz, *Lorenzo Vallas Schrift*, pp. 46–47 (quotes Gray, without dealing with the accuracy of her remark).

16. On all this, see A. Perosa's lucid and learned essay, "L'edizione veneta di Quintiliano coi commenti del Valla, di Pomponio Leto e di Sulpizio da Veroli," in *Miscellanea Augusto Campana* (Padua, 1981), 2:575–610.

17. See *Laurentii Valle epistole*, pp. 216, 279, 296–97, 306.

18. "Sed hoc ipsum argumenta ex causa trahit, si forte aut incredibile est id actum esse quod tabulae continent, aut, ut frequentius evenit, aliis probationibus aeque inartificialibus solvitur, si aut is in quem signatum est aut aliquis signator dicitur afuisse vel prius esse defunctus, si tempora non congruunt, si vel antecedentia vel insequentia tabulis repugnant. Inspectio etiam ipsa saepe falsum deprendit" (Quintilian *Institutio Oratoria*, ed. M. Winterbottom, 1 [Oxford 1970], 5.5.1).

19. See *Laurentii Valle epistole*, pp. 214–17 (letter to Giovanni Tortelli). On Valla's notes to *Parisinus latinus* 7723, see L. Cesarini Martinelli, "Le postille di Valla all'*Institutio Oratoria* di Quintiliano," in *Lorenzo Valla e l'umanesimo italiano*, ed. O. Besomi and M. Regoliosi

(Padua, 1986), pp. 21–50; on the posthumous publication of the notes, see A. Perosa, "L'edizione veneta di Quintiliano."

20. See also Cicero's mention of *Tabulae* in *De oratore* 2.27.115. On this topic, see L. de Sarlo, "La produzione dei documenti nel processo romano classico (procedura formulare e *cognitio extra ordinem*)," *Rendiconti dell'Istituto Lombardo* 70 (1937): 169–84; and L. de Sarlo, *Il documento oggetto dei rapporti giuridici privati* (Florence, 1935).

21. See O. Angermann, *De Aristotele rhetorum auctore*, diss. (Leipzig, 1904), who tried to identify the sources (above all, Caecilius of Calacte) of the "Aristotelian" passages in Quintilian. Cf. F. Solmsen, "The Aristotelian Tradition," p. 199–200 (cited in full at note 23 below). In his commentary on the *Institutio Oratoria* ("Belles Lettres," vol. 3, books 4 and 5 [Paris 1976], pp. 97ff.), J. Cousin, who rejects the possibility of a direct connection with Aristotle, admits that Quintilian's vocabulary is often close to Aristotle's, although the perspective is different.

22. The most relevant exception is provided by Chaïm Perelman and L. Olbrechts-Tyteca, *Traité de l'argumentation: La nouvelle rhétorique* (Paris 1958), whose approach is explicitly labeled a return to Aristotle. Aristotle is also invoked (in partial disagreement with Perelman) by M. Pera, *Scienza e retorica* (Bari, 1991).

23. See F. Solmsen, "The Aristotelian Tradition in Ancient Rhetoric" (1941), in *Kleine Schriften* (Hildesheim, 1968), 2:178–215; F. Solmsen, "Aristotle and Cicero on the Orator's Playing upon the Feelings" (1938), in *Kleine Schriften*, 2:216–30.

24. See G. Kennedy, *The Art of Rhetoric in the Roman World, 300 B.C–A.D. 300* (Princeton, 1972), pp. 114–15, 221–22; for a different view, see F. Solmsen, "Aristotle and Cicero," pp. 227–28.

25. See Solmsen, "Aristotle and Cicero," p. 216.

26. See, however, M. Regoliosi, "Lorenzo Valla e la concezione della storia," in *La storiografia umanistica* (Messina, 1987).

27. L. Valla, *Gesta Ferdinandi regis Aragonum*, ed. O. Besomi, (Padua, 1973), p. 7: "Nonne igitur ad huiusmodi veritatem eruendam historico opus est non minori accuratione ac sagacitate, quam aut iudici in deprehendendo vero ac iusto, aut medico in pervidendo morbo atque curando?" See A. Momigliano, "History Between Medicine and Rhetoric," *Ottavo contributo alla storia degli studi classici e del mondo antico* (Rome, 1987), pp. 13–25; see also my "Clues," and *Il giudice e lo storico*. For the recent bibliography, see P. Butti de Lima, *L'inchiesta e la prova. Immagine storiografica, pratica giuridica e retorica nella Grecia classica* (Turin, 1996).

28. See L. Valla, *Gesta Ferdinandi regis Aragonum*, p. 3: "et si plerique conditores oratorie artis, que historie mater est . . ." See, on the contrary, Momigliano, "History Between Medicine and Rhetoric."

29. J. Mabillon, *De re diplomatica* (Lutetiae Parisiorum [Paris], 1681), p. 23.

30. See M. Tavoni, "Lorenzo Valla e il volgare," in *Lorenzo Valla e l'umanesimo italiano: Atti del convegno internazionale di studi umanistici (Parma 18–19 ottobre 1984)*, ed. O. Besomi and M. Regoliosi (Padua, 1986), pp. 199–216.

31. See Biondo Flavio, *Scritti inediti e rari*, ed. B. Nogara (Rome, 1927), pp. 115–30 ("De verbis Romanae locutionis"); L. Bruni Arretini, *Epistolarum libri VIII . . .*, ed. L. Mehus (Florence, 1741), 2:62–68 book 6, letter 10, to Biondo Flavio. On this debate, see M. Tavoni, *Latino, grammatica, volgare. Storia di una questione umanistica* (Padua, 1984), pp. 3–41.

32. See Leonardo Bruni Aretino, *Humanistisch-philosophische Schriften*, ed. H. Baron (Leipzig, 1928; reprint 1969), pp. 81–96, especially pp. 85–86, 93, 95.

33. Ibid., p. 83.

34. Ibid., p. 86.

35. On replicas, for much evidence from a later period, see *Maestri e botteghe: Pittura a Firenze alla fine del Quattrocento*, ed. M. Gegori, A. Paolucci, and C. Acidini Luchinat (Milan, 1992).

36. See O. Kurz, *Fakes*, 2nd ed. (New York, 1967); *Fake? The Art of Deception*, ed. M. Jones (London, 1990), especially on later periods. Many challenging ideas can be found in *Retaining the Original: Multiple Originals, Copies, and Reproduction*, Studies in the History of Art, 20 (Washington, D.C., 1989).

37. See A. Grafton, *Forgers and Critics: Creativity and Duplicity in Western Scholarship* (Princeton, 1990).

38. See L. Valla, *Orazione per l'inaugurazione dell'anno accademico 1455–1456*, new critical ed. by S. Rizzo (Rome, 1994); W. J. Connell, "Lorenzo Valla: A Symposium. Introduction," *Journal of the History of Ideas* 57 (1996): 1ff.

39. See Quintilian, *Institutio oratoria*, 1.6.3: "Consuetudo vero certissima loquendi magistra, utendumque plane sermone, ut nummo, cui pubblica forma est" (see Tavoni, *Latino*, p. 265; cf. Valla, *Elegantiarum latinae linguae*, proemium).

40. "Et enim post collapsum imperium qui in grammatica, dialectica, rhetorica nisi nugas scripsit? quis orator hoc dignus nomine extitit? quis historicus, poeta, iurisconsultus, philosophus, theologus ulli veterum comparandus? Parum dico: nonne apud plerasque nationes tam in iudiciis quam extra iudicia scribitur illitterate, id est non latine? nonne singule pene civitates suum ius civile vernacula lingua condiderunt? Quod cum fit, quid aliud quam ius civile romanum exterminatur et pro nihilo habetur? Ita dum lingua latina abiicitur, omnes propemodum cum illa liberales abiiciuntur artes, ut licet videre ex Asia atque Africa, ex quibus quia lingua latina cum imperio eiecta est, ideo omnes bone artes pariter eiecte sunt et pristina barbaries rediit in possessionem. Quo cur in Europa non contingit? Nempe, ut reddam quod tertium est quod initio promisi, quia id fieri sedes apostolica prohibuit. Cuius rei sine dubio caput et causa extitit religio christiana" (Valla, *Orazione*, p. 198). Valla's text is not mentioned in D. Hay, *Europe: The Emergence of an Idea* (Edinburgh, 1957). Pope Pius II, who spoke of Europe on several occasions, for instance in his letter to Mehemet II (see pp. 83ff.), was clearly aware of Valla's text.

41. D. Cantimori (*Eretici italiani*, p. 56) sees a connection between Erasmus's translation and Valla's reflections on *sermo*.

3 Alien Voices

The Dialogic Element in Early Modern Jesuit Historiography

I

In the last three decades the cross-fertilization between history and anthropology has produced much exciting research on both sides. Recently the relationships between the two disciplines have often involved a third partner as well: literary theory. "Narrative functions," "authorial points of view," or "implicit readers" (along with some more arcane notions) have become increasingly familiar to both historians and anthropologists. This *ménage à trois* is a welcome event, although its products have been rather ambiguous thus far. Texts are often seen as worlds in themselves, as literary artifacts whose relationship to extratextual realities we are not entitled to explore. These skeptical conclusions do not take into consideration what seems obvious: that a deeper and farther-reaching awareness of the literary and rhetorical dimensions of a text can provide a more solid basis to the referential ambitions shared in the past by both history and anthropology.

This case study will focus on a long passage taken from a book published in Paris in the year 1700: the *Histoire des Isles Marianes, nouvellement converties à la Religion chrestienne; et de la mort glorieuse des premiers Missionnaires qui y ont prêché la Foy (History of the Marianas Islands, recently converted to the Christian Religion, and of the glorious death of the first Missionaries who preached the faith there)*. Its author, the French Jesuit Charles Le Gobien, was a remarkable man. As director (*procureur*) of the missions to China, he published in 1698 a book entitled *L'Histoire de l'édit de l'Empereur de la Chine en faveur de la religion Chrétienne*, a text that helped to ignite the famous controversy over "Chinese rites," the bold experiment made by the Jesuit missionaries to accommodate themselves to Chinese society. In an appendix to his book, Le Gobien defended the Jesuits' favorable attitude toward Chinese ceremonies, including "the honor paid by the Chinese to Confucius and to the dead."[1] Moreover, between 1702 and 1708, the year of his death, Le Gobien edited the first eight issues of the *Lettres édifiantes et curieuses*, a series of letters sent to Paris by French Jesuit missionaries from all over the world, which had a deep impact throughout Europe.[2]

In the following passage, Le Gobien describes the early stage of a failed attempt made by natives in 1685 to overthrow the Spanish settlers, who in 1565 had taken possession of the Mariana Islands, the archipelago located to the east of the Philippines.[3] Five years later, a young Spaniard, who had been cutting wood in the forest in order to make crosses, was killed under mysterious circumstances. Natives from the capital of Guam, the main island in the Marianas, were arrested, imprisoned, and then released. The atmosphere became tense. A nobleman, named Hurao, urged his fellow natives, through some artful speeches (*des discours étudiez*), to rise up against the Europeans and expel them from the Islands. Hurao's words, as Le Gobien reported them, were as follows:

Those Europeans should have stayed home. We did not need their help to be happy. We had what our Islands gave us; we relied on that, we did not want anything else. The knowledge they gave us made our needs bigger, our desires sharper. They complain because we have no clothing. If clothing had been necessary, Nature would have provided it for us. Why should we wear clothing? Is it not a useless object? Why should we encumber our arms and legs, pretending to cover them? They think we are simpletons; they look on us as Barbarians. But should we believe them? Is it not clear enough that, by pretending to teach us and polish our customs, they are corrupting us? That they spoil that first simplicity in which we used to live? That they take away our freedom, which we should cherish more than life? They want to persuade us that they make us happy; several among you are blind enough to trust their words. But how can we believe this, when we see that since these foreigners came to corrupt and destroy our peace we have been afflicted by all kinds of misfortunes and illnesses? Before their arrival in our Islands, did we ever hear anything about those insects that so cruelly torment us? Did we ever know rats, mice, flies, mosquitoes, and all those small animals that exist only to plague us? Here you see the nice presents they gave us, brought to us by their floating machines! Before their arrival, did we ever hear about colds and flus? When we were sick, we had remedies; they brought us illnesses and no remedies at all. Why should we sink into these great miseries, seduced by our cupidity, by our unhappy desire for iron objects and similar trifles, whose value is generated only by our own appreciation?

They blame our poverty, our ignorance, our clumsiness. But what are they looking for among us, if we are so poor as they say? Believe me, if they did not need us, they would not expose themselves, as they do, to so many risks; they would not make so many efforts to settle themselves among us. The purpose of their teaching is to convince us to imitate their customs, to follow their laws, to lose the invaluable freedom we have inherited from our fathers: in a word, to make us unhappy by craving an imaginary happiness—a happiness one can enjoy only when one no longer exists.

They regard our histories as fables and fictions. Are we not entitled to say the same about what they teach us, asking us to believe it as an incontestable truth? They take advantage of our simplicity and good faith. They use their cleverness only to deceive us; their science, only to make us unhappy. They are right in convincing us that we are ignorant and blind, in so far as we realized too late how pernicious their designs were, and how wrong we were to have allowed them to settle among us. Let us not lose our courage in looking at our unhappiness. They are just a handful of people: we can easily get rid of them. We lack their killing weapons, which spread terror and death everywhere, but we can overcome them by our number. We are stronger than we think; in a short time we can easily free ourselves from these foreigners, retrieving our pristine freedom.[4]

These words, Le Gobien goes on, made a sudden impact on the natives, many of whom took up their weapons and prepared to attack the Spaniards. After a few violent encounters the revolt was crushed in a matter of days.

II

The eloquence of Hurao's harangue (one among several included in Le Gobien's *Histoire*) is undeniable. Seventy years later it inspired, as has been suggested, the Old Man's harangue in Diderot's *Supplement au voyage de Bougainville*.[5] To a late-twentieth-century reader it may sound like a foretaste of many subsequent denouncements of European cultural imperialism. The same late-twentieth-century reader will also take for granted that (1) the harangue does not reproduce the words that Hurao might have uttered on that occasion; and (2) the inclusion of such a harangue in a historical work would be totally inappropriate today, not to say absurd.[6] But we must ask, how were these issues perceived in 1700?

The inclusion of harangues allegedly delivered by non-Europeans in historical works raised doubts among Jesuit scholars beginning in the late-sixteenth century. In the process of collecting material for his *Historia natural y moral de las Indias*, José de Acosta received a manuscript designated as *Historia mexicana* from a fellow Jesuit, Juan de Tovar. Acosta wrote to Tovar with three questions: was the work reliable? how could the Indians, who had no writing, have preserved the memory of so many different things? and finally, "How could the speeches or harangues included in that history be ascribed (as the history claims) to some ancient rhetoricians, since in the absence of literacy it seems impossible that those long and, in their genre, elegant speeches could have been preserved?" Tovar replied that the Indian boys "who were trained as rhetoricians" used to learn the most famous speeches by heart. The answer sounded so convincing that Acosta included it in his *Historia natural y moral de las Indias*.[7] Jesuit missionaries to Canada did not hesitate to compare the harangues delivered by Indians to Livy.[8] After all, rhetoric—as Aristotle wrote at the very beginning of his treatise on this topic—deals, like its counterpart, dialectic, "with matters that are in a manner within the cognizance of all men and not confined to any special science" (1354a).[9]

Some decades later, the inclusion of harangues in historical writings began to be debated on a more theoretical level. The Italian Jesuit Agostino Mascardi, in his influential treatise *Dell'arte historica*, published in Rome in 1636, wrote that the "example of the whole of Antiquity, which today is accepted as law" left no doubt that harangues could be legitimately included in historical works.[10] But the detailed analysis that paved the way for Mascardi's conclusion showed that Greek and Roman historians had, on the contrary, rather divergent attitudes toward harangues. Forty years later another Jesuit, the French René Rapin, stressed the disagreement "among our Masters" before suggesting a prudent rejection of "those formal harangues, delivered in front of an army or before a battle, [of] those boring and lengthy discussions." "In the most sensible historical works," he concluded, "they have nearly fallen out of use (*ne sont presque plus d'usage*)," usually being superseded by indirect speeches.[11] In fact, the debate went on for decades.[12] In 1700, the year in which Le Gobien published his *Histoire des Isles Marianes*, Hurao's harangue was already out of fashion.

Let us analyze it on a purely formal level, leaving aside for the moment the issue of its referential value. The actual content of

Hurao's allocution is less important than the mold in which it was cast: the leader of a conspiracy, addressing his followers on the eve of a crucial battle. Here we may be tempted to detect, behind Hurao, an ancient model—Catiline, the archenemy of Roman oligarchy and negative hero of Sallust's *De coniuratione Catilinae*.[13]

The portrait of Hurao sketched by Le Gobien follows, in its contradictory qualities, the pattern set by Sallust: that of "a clever man," who "was much more intelligent and able than Barbarians usually are"; a man who "had gained such authority among the people and the nobility that he was regarded as an oracle"; who, having become "a sworn enemy of the missionaries," rejected the presents made to him by the Jesuit Sanvitores, which only increased his "pride and insolence." "His only desire was to create trouble, to incite a revolt against the Spaniards."[14]

In the seventeenth century, Sallust had become immensely popular. In 1675 the anonymous editor of a French translation of Sallust's works compared him to Tacitus, his great disciple, both for "narration, which is the body, and political education, which is the soul" of history.[15] The impact of Sallust's *De coniuratione Catilinae* can be detected in *La congiura del Conte Gio. Luigi de' Fieschi* written by Agostino Mascardi, the Italian Jesuit (which was later translated and reworked by Cardinal de Retz), as well as in the *Conjuration des Espagnols contre la Republique de Venise en l'année M.DC.XVIII* by César de Saint-Réal, who also had a Jesuit education.[16] Part of Sallust's appeal came from his use of harangues. Catiline's allocution to his followers was so famous that Paolo Beni, professor of rhetoric at the University of Padua, took it as a starting point for a theoretical discussion on the role of harangues in historical writings.[17]

Harangues, compared by their defenders to a rhetorical ornament, tended to multiply, like ornaments in baroque churches. They are possibly too long and too frequent, Mascardi wrote in a semiapologetic tone introducing his work on the Fieschi conspiracy, but in the long run they contributed to the work's success. The lengthy title of a composite volume published in London in 1678 reads: *A collection of select discourses out of the most eminent wits of France and Italy. A preface to Monsieur Sarasin's works by Monsieur Pelisson. A dialogue of love. Wallenstein's conspiracy, by Mr. Sarrasin. Alcidalis, a romance, by Mr. Voiture. Fieski's conspiracy, by Signor Mascardi.* This strange mixture of

history and romance suggests that the role of harangues in historical works was related to a much larger issue. Mascardi had perceptively interpreted harangues, both in historiography and in judicial rhetoric, as conjectural efforts aimed at discerning the truth.
At stake, he insisted, was the role of verisimilitude within historical writing. The issue went back to Aristotle, who in his *Poetics*
had connected history to truth and poetry to verisimilitude.[18]
Retrospectively, we can see that the final disappearance of harangues from historiography implied nothing less than a global re-
shuffling of the boundaries between history and fiction. This
meant (1) the emergence of the historical novel; (2) the birth of the
history of manners (*histoire de moeurs*); and (3) the fusion of antiquarianism and *histoire philosophique* which led to historiography in the modern sense of the word.[19] Our case study is merely a
small episode in a much larger and longer story.

III

Let us go back again to our original text: a harangue pronounced
by a leader of a conspiracy. Such a topic had multiple resonances
to a seventeenth-century reader. "Conspiracies," wrote Saint-Réal
at the beginning of his work on the Marquis of Bedmar's 1618 attempt to overthrow the Venetian Republic, "are the greatest of all
human enterprises . . . the most moral and instructive among historical topics."[20] In the age of European absolutism, conspiracies
provided an invaluable opportunity for scrutinizing political
power and the roots of its legitimacy, as well as the tragic isolation
of the individual who dared to challenge it.[21]

The leader of a conspiracy is a tragic hero whose values and
ideals are not always shared by the historian. Here the potential of
the harangue as a rhetorical device emerges. "The historian,"
Mably commented in his *De la manière d'écrire l'histoire* (1783),
"will successfully put in the mouth of his characters something
that would shock in his own."[22] Through his hero—an antihero, a
villain—the historian will set up the argument against his own be-
liefs and convictions. He will launch an attack against legitimate
power, providing reasons for overthrowing it.

All this must have appealed to the theatrical sensibilities of the
Jesuits, to their bold speculations on the nature of political power

(which included even regicide) and to their attitude toward cultural diversity.[23] This point needs some further clarification.

IV

In his *Problems of Dostoevsky's Poetics* (1929), Mikhail Bakhtin, the great Russian critic, made a distinction between monologic (or monophonic) texts, dominated by a more or less concealed authorial voice, and dialogic (or polyphonic) texts, staging a clash of contradictory world views in which the author takes no sides. Plato's dialogues and Dostoevsky's novels were, according to Bakhtin, prominent examples of the latter. Nobody would think for a moment of putting in this company a narrative written from a hagiographic perspective such as Le Gobien's *Histoire des Isles Marianes*. However, expressing the point of view of the natives through Hurao's distinct voice can be regarded as a deliberate attempt to create a dissonance, adding a dialogic dimension to a basically monologic narrative.

The dialogic dimension here seems to have sprung directly from the striking attitude toward cultural diversity adopted by Jesuit missionaries. In order to spread the faith of Christ they consciously decided to accommodate themselves to all kinds of customs: from the caste system in India to the cult of ancestors in China. The polemical hedge of this missionary strategy is stressed over and over in the *Lettres édifiantes et curieuses*. Those who lived "in India as they live in France, in England, in Holland, without restraining themselves or accommodating, as far as they could, to the customs of the Indian people," had discredited the European name in the eyes of the natives.[24]

The urge to avoid what we would today call "ethnocentric prejudice" inspired the protoethnographic approach displayed by the Jesuits in the letters they sent from their Asian or American missions. In 1720 Father du Halde, the successor of Le Gobien as editor of the *Lettres édifiantes*, stressed the superiority of the Jesuit missionaries living in India over "those who travel for curiosity or trade." The latter knew only the coastal places; the former became in a sense like natives (*sont comme naturalisez parmi eux*); they learn the natives' language, developing a deep knowledge of their manners, laws, and customs.[25] "And unto the Jews I became as a

Jew, that I might gain the Jews": the words Paul addressed to the Corinthians (1 *Corinthians* 9:19–23) were developed by a colleague of Le Gobien, Father Louis Le Comte, into a justification of the Jesuit missionary strategy, based upon religious accommodation:

One must be barbarous with the barbarians and polished with civilized people; one must lead an ordinary life in Europe and a deeply austere life among the penitents of India; one must be well dressed in China and half naked in the forests of Madurai: in this way the uniform and unchanging gospel will be more easily insinuated into the spirits.[26]

But a word like "barbarous" had deeply ambivalent associations for the Jesuits. In 1715 Father de Mailla sent a letter describing the island of Taiwan.[27] "So far this land," he wrote, "has been inhabited by a barbarous, uncivilized population [*un peuple barbare et nullement policé*]; horses, rams, goats, even pigs (which are common in mainland China) are very rare here." But in commenting on the local matrilocal custom, which decreed that the groom should join the bride's household, de Mailla remarked: "their marriages are not barbarous at all" (*leurs mariages n'ont rien de barbare*). Brides are not sold as they are in China, he explained; financial considerations, so important in Europe, do not play any role in Taiwan; parents are not involved in the marriage. De Mailla spoke with enthusiasm about the effects of matrilocality: in Taiwan daughters are deeply appreciated because "they can acquire sons-in-law who will support one's old age." In the same letter he mentioned that a wave of revolts against the Chinese government had broken out in Taiwan. De Mailla had expressed his concern to a Chinese Mandarin who had just been appointed viceroy of one of the Taiwanese provinces: "He replied in a cold manner: 'My Father, so much the worse for these barbarous people, if they prefer to remain in their barbarity; we are trying to transform them into human beings; they resist, so much the worse for them; nothing is perfect.'" These words caused the Jesuit to comment: "They can certainly be considered barbarous according to some rules prevailing in the Chinese world; however, they are, I believe, much closer to the true Philosophy than the great majority of the most famous Chinese philosophers."[28] They are meek and fair, he explained, respectful of hierarchies, chaste, and so on.

"Closer to the true Philosophy": these words could have been spoken by that famous pupil of the Jesuits, Voltaire. As Werner

Kaegi has remarked, the vision of world history so powerfully displayed in the *Essai sur les moeurs* was clearly indebted to the Jesuit missionaries, and we may add, to the enterprise started by Le Gobien half a century earlier.[29] But it is the intellectual ancestry of the *Lettres édifiantes et curieuses*, not their posterity, that concerns us here.

V

In his famous essay "On Cannibals" (1.31), Montaigne explored the ambiguities of the notion of barbarity, suggesting that the Brazilian natives were sometimes not barbarous at all, for instance in their poetry; they were less barbarous than the civilized Europeans, and truly barbarous and savage only in so far as they were closer to nature.[30] The reflections of Father de Mailla on the inhabitants of Taiwan seem to follow Montaigne's intricate lead, with the Chinese taking the role of the Europeans and "true Philosophy" the role of nature. This is not an isolated convergence. The text by Le Gobien with which we began turns around the topic of another essay by Montaigne, that "Of the Custom of Wearing Clothes" (1.36): the conflict between nakedness and the wearing of clothing, the natural and the artificial. Again a passage from Hurao's harangue:

They [the Europeans] complain because we have no clothing. If clothing had been necessary, Nature would have provided it for us. Why should we wear clothing? Is it not a useless object? Why should we encumber our arms and legs, pretending to cover them? They think we are simpletons; they look on us as Barbarians. But should we believe them? Is it not clear enough that, by pretending to teach us and polish our customs, they are corrupting us? That they spoil that first simplicity in which we used to live? That they take our freedom, which we should cherish more than life?

What we are hearing is the voice of "those nations who are said to be still living in the sweet freedom of Nature's first laws"—as Montaigne called them. The Jesuit missionaries left Europe with Montaigne's *Essays*, if not in their pockets, at least in their minds. Montaigne provided a framework, a schema with which to understand information about newly discovered lands and people. "Notwithstanding their poverty, they are happy and satisfied with their fate" (*ils sont gais et contens de leur sort*), said a letter, republished by Le Gobien in the first issue of his *Lettres édifiantes et curieuses*, which described the life of the inhabitants of the Palau Islands (not far from the Mariana archipelago).[31] In his *Histoire des Isles Marianes*, Le Gobien himself turned the arguments of Montaigne into a harangue, and the unnamed "noble savage" into Hurao, the nobleman from the Mariana Islands, full of hatred for European civilization.

In this rhetorical shift Le Gobien may have relied upon a celebrated page from another Roman historian, Tacitus. The harangue delivered by Calgacus, the Caledonian chieftain, on the eve of the battle against Agricola, is a powerful denouncement of Roman imperialism.[32] Justus Linsius praised it in his commentary as "a brave and noble speech" (*animosa et alta oratio*).[33] Though it may contain echoes of Sallust, it seems much closer to Hurao's harangue than Catiline's. Calgacus claimed that his people "had never seen the shores of slavery and had preserved our very eyes from the desecration and contamination of tyranny."[34] Hurao's emphasis on freedom ("our pristine freedom," "the invaluable freedom we have inherited from our fathers") appears to be indebted to the immaculate freedom of the ancient Britons, celebrated by Tacitus, as well as to the "sweet freedom of Nature's first laws," which Montaigne had found among the Brazilian natives.

The affinity between Montaigne's pedagogical (or antipedagogical) ideas and the Jesuit educational system has already been noticed by such authoritative scholars as Pierre Villey and François de Dainville.[35] But after 1676, when the *Essays* were put on the Index of Prohibited Books, Montaigne circulated among the Jesuits in indirect form, as the case of Saint-Réal's *De l'usage de l'histoire* shows. The author of such works as the book on the Bedmar conspiracy mentioned earlier, and the "historical novella" which inspired Schiller's *Dom Carlos*, Saint-Réal would today be placed in a gray area at the intersection between fiction and history.[36] The seven short essays of *De l'usage de l'histoire*, first published in 1671, were reprinted several times, and finally included in the *Méthode pour étudier l'histoire*, a two-volume collective enterprise issued by the Jesuit order (*aux dépens de la Compagnie*) in 1714.[37] The presence in the work of a writer of such stature as the Jesuit René Rapin presumably gave credibility to the very unconventional text by Saint-Réal, which Bayle judged to be "full of original and sensible thoughts."[38] The fifth essay opens in a truly

Montaignesque spirit: "Everybody knows that customs change."
The example with which Saint-Réal begins is a small anecdote: in
Paris, one hundred years before, new magistrates were compelled
to shave their beards before assuming their office. The custom,
Saint-Réal remarks, seems "bizarre," even unreasonable: all civilized people, including ancient Greeks and Romans, always regarded long beards as a sign of majesty, gravity, wisdom. But from
this *bizarrerie*, Saint-Réal goes on, some relevant implications can
be drawn. Beards cannot be regarded as a natural sign of majesty,
because "every natural idea must be universal both in time and
space, with no exception."[39] But Saint-Réal disagrees with the *esprits forts* who believe that custom is everything:

> they exult in collecting the strangest habits and uses from the New World,
> Peru, and China, because they pretend that human beings are ruled only
> by opinion, that Nature does not play any role: as if the burgeoning reason
> of those semibeastly populations could be legitimately compared with
> ours, which has been polished by a long accumulation of science and edu-
> cation, as well as by the knowledge of every trace of civilization on
> earth![40]

Against the libertines who argue for "the general uncertainty of
everything," Saint-Réal emphasizes the role of reason; revelation
is never mentioned. Above all, he insists, one must refrain from
"the vice of singularity," the desire to be different. The implicit
conclusion was clear enough: one must accommodate oneself to
the prevailing customs—either in India or in France. Saint-Réal's
polemical remarks against the radical skepticism of the erudite
libertines should not deceive us. He was in a way one of them
himself, as the last essay of his *De l'usage de l'histoire* clearly
shows. Saint-Réal boldly discussed the well-known libertine topic
of religion as fraud (*l'imposture des religions*), starting with Zo-
roaster and Numa, and ending with Louis XI of France and his cyn-
ical use of the Christian faith. The presence of such a text in a
quasi-official volume, published "at the expenses of the Jesuit
Order," is surprising—and revealing.[41]

VI

It would be absurd to suggest that Le Gobien identified himself
with the Montaignesque language of Hurao's harangue. The targets

of the native revolt were the Europeans, among them the Jesuits. Le Gobien lent to Hurao the ideas about pristine freedom and simplicity he had learned from Montaigne because he wanted to be rhetorically effective. He was not using harangues as part of a deliberate strategy, as G. Bonnot de Mably suggested nearly a century later: "the historian will go back under a borrowed mask to the first principles of the natural law, and will explain under which conditions Nature allows societies to be happy."[42] But through Hurao's harangue Le Gobien expressed an inner ambiguity about European civilization, as well as, more indirectly, some of his (and his order's) deepest thoughts about religion and society.

In *L'Histoire de l'édit de l'Empereur de la Chine en faveur de la religion Chrétienne*, published by Le Gobien two years before the *Histoire des Isles Marianes*, one could find, among other things, that "China kept for more than two thousand years the knowledge of the true God, and only became idolatrous five or six hundred years before the birth of Jesus Christ"; a view shared by Matteo Ricci, the first Jesuit missionary to China.[43] The Theological Faculty of Paris put this sentence on a list of condemned opinions concerning "Chinese rites." One of them, taken from Louis Le Comte's *Nouveaux Mémoires sur l'etat présent de la Chine*, read: "If Judaea had the advantage of consecrating a more rich and magnificent temple to God, sanctified by the presence and the prayers of Our Redeemer, China had a not small glory in sacrificing to the Creator, in the most ancient temple of the Universe."[44]

The same order that had been in the forefront of the Catholic Counter-Reformation seemed to belittle the Redemption; the same order that had built hundreds of churches inspired by the gorgeous Chiesa del Gesù in Rome exalted a presumably primitive temple built by a Chinese emperor many centuries before Christ.[45] The reaction of the Dominican Friars of the Theological Faculty of Paris, confronted with the Jesuit paradox, was predictably harsh.[46] In 1704 Pope Clement XI condemned the Society of Jesus; forty years later the debate over the "Chinese rites" came to an end.

VII

Sallust, Tacitus, Montaigne: the multiple threads identified within the fabric of Hurao's harangue can help us to analyze Le

Gobien's rhetoric. Hurao turns out to be a projection of Le Gobien; the dialogue actually a concealed monologue—with one relevant exception. It is a footnote, a comment on the passage of Hurao's harangue:

But how can we believe this [the promise of happiness the Europeans made to us], when we see that since these foreigners came to corrupt and destroy our peace we have been afflicted by all kinds of misfortunes and illnesses? Before their arrival to our Islands, did we ever hear anything about those insects that so cruelly torment us? Did we ever know rats, mice, flies, mosquitoes, and all those small animals that exist only to plague us? Here you see the nice presents they gave us, brought to us by their floating machines! Before their arrival, did we ever hear about colds and flus?

And here is Le Gobien's footnote:

We have some difficulty in believing that the inhabitants of those Islands never suffered from colds or flus, and that before the arrival of the Spaniards there were no insects in those Islands. It is certain, however, that these Barbarians accused the Spaniards of this as if it were a crime, often reproaching them for it.[47]

Hurao's attack against the Europeans for the pestilences they brought with them was expressed—as was the rest of his harangue—in language provided by Le Gobien. But the latter's ironical footnote points to a distance, elsewhere absent, between the author and his text. For a moment Le Gobien seems unable to understand what he has written.[48] Behind the smooth rhetoric of Le Gobien's narrative, we hear at last a different, dissonant, untamed voice: an alien voice, coming from a place outside the text.

This internal evidence is confirmed by some external testimony as well. Up to now, we have refrained from examining the sources of Le Gobien's narrative. He never traveled to the Marianas. Besides Francisco García's *Vida y martirio del venerable padre Diego Luis de Sanvitores, de la compañía de Jesús, primer apóstol de las islas Marianas* (Madrid, 1683), he relied heavily upon the yearly letters sent by the Jesuit fathers of the Philippine Province.[49] From them he gathered the details about the natives' revolt, including a passage concerning "a great personage named Hurao," who had been apprehended as one of the main instigators of the troubles, and later released.[50] There is no further information about him in the Jesuits' letters. What they mention, instead, is the natives' belief that "rats, flies, mosquitoes, and all kinds of illnesses were brought by the ships coming to the islands."[51]

As we have seen, Le Gobien ridiculed this belief. Today, ecologists are not so amused. "The rats are coming . . . at the rate of six or seven island invasions a year every year since 1841, at one count," the *Los Angeles Times* reported on 17 May 1993. And, again, "Through commerce and fishing, exploration and military maneuvers, we have spread rats to 82% of the world's islands, according to federal scientists."[52]

It would have been most reassuring to analyze authorial strategies from behind the protective walls of a single text. From that in perspective to speak about a reality "out there" would naturally have been a positivistic naiveté. But texts have leaks. Through the leak we have discovered, something unexpected emerges: the armies of rats invading the world, the other face of our civilization.

Notes

1. C. Le Gobien, *Histoire de l'édit de l'Empereur de la Chine en faveur de la religion Chrétienne, avec un éclaircissement sur les honneurs que les Chinois rendent à Confucius et aux morts* (Paris, 1698) (an Italian translation was published immediately after). On the Chinese attitude toward the Christian missionaries, cf. J. Gernet, *Chine et Christianisme* (Paris, 1982) (I used the Italian translation [Casale Monferrato, 1984], with an introduction by A. Prosperi).

2. Cf. *Lettres édifiantes et curieuses, écrites des missions étrangères, nouvelle édition, Mémoires d'Amérique*, vol. 6 (Toulouse, 1810), p. xxvii: "Le Père le Gobien est l'Editeur des huit premières tomes; il écrivait avec goût, et avec cette facilité que donne l'étude profonde et réfléchie des grandes modèles, et joignait aux excellentes qualités de son esprit, les vertus les plus rares et les plus précieuses. Le Père Duhalde lui succéda . . . " See A. Rétif, S.J., "Brève histoire des `Lettres édifiantes et curieuses,'" *Neue Zeitschrift für Missionswissenschaft—Nouvelle Revue de science missionnaire*, vol. 7 (1951), pp. 37–50.

3. For the date of the revolt, see F. Garzia, *Istoria della conversione alla nostra santa fede dell'Isole Mariane, dette prima de' Ladroni, nella vita, predicatione, e morte gloriosa per Christo del venerabile p. Diego Luigi di Sanvitores e d'altri suoi compagni della compagnia di Giesù . . ., scritta nell'idioma castigliano . . . e tradotta nell'italiano con l'accrescimento di notitie dal padre Ambrosio Ortiz della medesima Compagnia* (Naples, 1686), pp. 569ff. The Spanish edition had been published in Madrid, in 1683.

4. Cf. C. Le Gobien, de la Compagnie de Jésus, *Histoire des Isles Marianes . . .* (Paris, 1700), pp. 139–46. Two passages from this work are mentioned by S. Landucci, *I filosofi e i selvaggi (1580–1780)* (Bari, 1972) (see

index). Here is Le Gobien's text: "Ces Européans auroient bien fait, leur disoit-il, de demeurer dans leur païs. Nous n'avions pas besoin de leurs secours pour vivre heureux. Contens de ce que nos Isles fournissoient, nous nous en servions sans rien désirer au delà. Les connoissances qu'ils nous ont données, n'ont fait qu'augmenter nos besoins, et qu'irriter nos désirs. Ils trouvent mauvais que nous ne sommes pas vêtus. Si cela eust eté necessaire la nature y auroit pourvû. Pourquoy nous charger d'habits, puisque c'est une chose superfluë, et nous embarrasser les bras et les jambes sous pretexte de nous les couvrir? Ils nous traitent de gens grossiers, et il nous regardent comme des Barbares. Nous devons-nous les en croire? Ne voïons-nous pas que sous pretexte de nous instruire et de cultiver nos moeurs, il les corrompent; qu'il nous tirent de cette premiere simplicité dans laquelle nous vivions, et qu'il nous ostent enfin nostre liberté, qui nous doit estre plus chere que la vie? Ils veulent nous persuader qu'il nous rendent heureux, et plusieurs d'entre nous sont assez aveugles pour les en croire sur leur parole. Mais pourrions-nous avoir ces sentiments, si nous faisions reflexion que nous ne sommes accablez de miseres et de maladies que depuis ces étrangers sont venus nous désoler et troubler nostre repos? Avant leur arrivée dans ces Isles, sçavions-nous ce que c'estoit que toutes ces insectes qui nous persecutent si cruellement? Connoissions-nous les rats, les souris, les mouches, les mosquites, et tous ces autres petits animaux, qui ne sont au monde que pour nous tourmenter? Voilà les beaux presens qu'il nous ont faits, et que leur machines flotantes nous ont aportez! Avant eux sçavions-nous ce que c'estoit que rheumes et que fluxions? Si nous avions quelques maladies, nous avions des remedes pour nous en délivrer; au lieu qu'ils nous apportent leurs maux sans nous apprendre à les guérir. Falloit-il que nostre cupidité et le malheureux desir que nous avions d'avoir de fer et d'autres bagatelles, ausquelles la seule estime que nous en faisons, donne le prix, nous precipitast dans de si grands malheurs?

Ils nous reprochent nostre pauvreté, nostre ignorance et nostre peu d'adresse. Mais si nous sommes si pauvres qu'ils le disent, que viennent-ils chercher parmi nous? Croïez-moy, s'ils n'avoient pas besoin de nous, ils ne s'exposeroient pas comme ils font, à tant de perils, et ils ne feroient pas tant d'efforts pour s'établir parmi nous. A quoy aboutit ce qu'ils nous enseignent, qu'à nous faire prendre leurs coûtumes, qu'à nous assujetir à leurs loix, et qu'à nous faire perdre cette précieuse liberté que nos pères nous ont laissée: en un mot qu'à nous rendre malheureux sous l'esperance d'un chimerique bonheur, dont on ne peut joüir qu'après qu'on n'est plus?

Ils traitent nos histoires de fables et de fictions. N'avons-nous pas le mesme droit d'en dire autant de ce qu'ils nous enseignent, et de ce qu'ils nous proposent à croire comme des veritez incontestables? Ils s'abusent de nostre simplicité et de nostre bonne foy. Tout leur art ne va qu'à nous tromper, et toute leur science ne tend qu'à nous rendre malheureux. Si nous sommes ignorans et aveugles, comme ils voudroient nous le faire croire, c'est d'avoir connu trop tard leurs pernicieux desseins, et d'avoir souffert qu'ils se soient établis parmi nous. Ne perdons pas courage à la

vûë de nos malheurs. Ils ne sont encore qu'une poignée de gens, nous pouvons aisément nous en défaire. Si nous n'avons pas ces armes meurtrieres,
qui portent la terreur et la mort par tout, nous sommes en estat de les ac-
cabler par le nombre et par la multitude. Nous sommes plus forts que
nous ne pensons, et nous pouvons en peu de temps nous délivrer de ces
étrangers, et nous remettre dans notre première liberté."

   5. D. Diderot, *Supplément au Voyage de Bougainville*, ed. G. Chinard
(Paris, 1935), pp. 118–19, n. 2. Chinard, who apologizes for the length of
the quotation, omitted one sentence from it: see below, notes 47 and 51.

   6. Roberto Longhi's tongue-in-cheek hypothetical (and indirect) dialogue between Masolino and Masaccio on the scaffoldings of the Ma-
donna del Carmine is one of the few exceptions that confirm the rule:
'*Fatti di Masolino e di Masaccio' e altri studi sul Quattrocento*, Complete
Works, vol. 7, tome 1 (Florence, 1975) p. 15.

   7. J. García Icazbalceta, *Don Fray Juan de Zumárraga Primer Obispo y
Arzobispo de México* (Mexico City, 1881), appendix, pp. 263–67. Tovar is
mentioned by J. de Acosta, *Historia natural y moral de las Indias* [1590],
ed. B. G. Beddall (Valencia, 1977), pp. 407ff. (bk. 6, ch. 1). I was unable to
see E. O'Gorman, "Fray Diego Durán, el padre Juan de Tovar y la Historia
natural y moral de las Indias del padre José de Acosta," in J. de Acosta, *Historia natural y moral de las Indias* (Mexico City, 1985), pp. lxxvi–xcv.

   8. Jean de Brebeuf, *Les relations de ce qui s'est passé au pays des Hu-
rons, 1635–1648*, ed. T. Besterman (Geneva, 1957), p. 152.

   9. Aristotle, *The "Art" of Rhetoric*, trans. J. H. Freese, The Loeb Classical Library (Cambridge, Mass., and London, 1972), 1.1.1.

   10. See A. Mascardi, *Dell'arte historica trattati cinque* (Rome, 1636),
pp. 142–51 (treatise 2, ch. 4).

   11. See R. Rapin, *Les Réflexions sur l'Histoire* (1677), in *Oeuvres* (Am-
sterdam, 1709), 2:269–72, especially p. 270.

   12. The issue was still regarded as worthy of discussion by Mably—a
philosopher, not a professional historian—in 1783: see the section from
his *De la manière d'écrire l'histoire*, republished under the title "L'historien, le romancier, le poète," *Poétique* 49 (February 1982): 5–8.

   13. See A. La Penna, "Il ritratto 'paradossale' da Silla a Petronio," *As-
petti del pensiero storico latino* (Turin, 1978), pp. 193–221, especially pp.
212–15. As Marx noticed on his copy of Machiavelli's *Istorie fiorentine*,
Sallust inspired the harangue allegedly delivered by the leader of the
Ciompi: see *Ex libris Karl Marx und Friedrich Engels*, ed. B. Kaiser and I.
Werchan (Berlin, 1967) p. 134, no. 286, as pointed out by G. Bock, "Machiavelli als Geschichtsschreiber," *Quellen und Forschungen aus italienis-
chen Archiven und Bibliotheken* 66 (1986): 153–90, especially pp. 175ff.

   14. Cf. Le Gobien, *Histoire des Isles Marianes*, pp. 137–38.

   15. *L'Histoire de la guerre des Romains contre Jugurta roy des Nu-
mides, et l'Histoire de la conjuration de Catilina. Ouvrages de Saluste
nouvellement traduits en François* (Paris, 1675), introduction: "On doit
considerer deux choses dans une Histoire, la Narration qui en est le corps,
et l'Instruction Politique qui en est l'âme." A list of the harangues is con-

veniently placed before the index. The addressee of the printing privilege, dated August 18, 1673, is a "sieur A. D. C. A. F." So far I have been unable to identify him.

16. See A. Mascardi, *La congiura del Conte Gio. Luigi de' Fieschi* (Venice, 1629); C. de Saint-Réal, *Conjuration des Espagnols contre la Republique de Venise en l'année M.DC.XVIII,* in *Oeuvres meslées . . ., nouv. éd. augmentée de sa critique* (Utrecht, 1693), pp. 215–329. On the latter, see G. Dulong, *L'abbé de Saint-Réal: Etude sur les rapports de l'histoire et du roman au XVIIe siècle* (Paris, 1921), 1:167–217. A perceptive critic recently remarked that Saint-Real's *Dom Carlos* is a "nouvelle d'une extraordinaire densité et dont la faible notoriété est une anomalie de l'histoire du goût" (T. Pavel, *L'art de l'éloignement: Essai sur l'imagination classique* [Paris, 1996], pp. 321–35, especially p. 321).

17. Pauli Benii Eugubini, *In Sallustii Catilinariam commentarii* (Venice, 1622), pp. 79ff.; see also, by the same author, *De historia libri quatuor* (Venice, 1622). See P. B. Diffley, *Paolo Beni* (Oxford, 1988).

18. See A. Mascardi, *Dell'arte historica,* p. 145.

19. Cf. A. Momigliano, "Ancient History and the Antiquarian," *Contributo alla storia degli studi classici* (Rome, 1979), pp. 67–106.

20. Saint-Réal, *Conjuration des Espagnols*: "De toutes les entreprises des hommes, il n'en est point de si grandes que les Conjurations. . . . Ces considérations m'ont toûjours fait regarder ces sortes d'entreprises comme les endroits de l'Histoire les plus moraux et les plus instructifs."

21. See F. Moretti, "La letteratura europea," in *Storia d'Europa* (Turin, 1993), 1: 841–46, for some inspiring remarks on tragedy and absolutism.

22. "L'historien mettra avec succès, dans la bouche des personnages qu'il fait parler, des choses qui choqueraient dans la sienne" (Bonnot de Mably, "L'historien, le romancier, le poète," p. 7).

23. On Jesuit theater, see the bibliography mentioned by J. W. O'Malley, *The First Jesuits* (Cambridge, Mass., 1993), p. 422, n. 118. On regicide, see the famous text by J. Mariana, *De rege et regis institutione, libri III* (Paris, 1611), pp. 51–68: 1.6 ("An tyrannum opprimere fas est") and 1.7 ("An liceat tyrannum veneno occidere").

24. Introduction by J. B. du Halde to *Lettres édifiantes et curieuses . . .,* X recueil (Paris, 1732): "Quoyque les autres Européans n'ignorassent pas la délicatesse des Indiens sur cet article [of castes], ils n'y ont pas eu plus d'égard que les Portugais; ils ont vécu aux Indes, comme ils vivent en France, en Angleterre, et en Hollande, sans se contraindre et sans s'accommoder, autant qu'il le pouvoient, aux usages de la Nation." See also P. Martin, letter to P. Le Gobien, *Lettres édifiantes et curieuses . . .,* V recueil (Paris, 1708), pp. 1ff., especially pp. 14, 17ff., 27–29; and, on a general level, the perceptive remarks made by J. W. O'Malley, *The First Jesuits,* pp. 255–56. On the notion of accommodation, see A. Funkenstein, *Theology and the Scientific Imagination* (Princeton, 1986), pp. 202–89; S. D. Benin, *The Footprints of God: Divine Accommodation in Jewish and Christian Thought* (Albany, 1993). On its relation to missionary activity, see J. Thauren, *Die Akkommodation in katholischen Heidenapostolat.*

Eine Missionstheoretische Studie (Münster in Westphalia, 1927); A. Prosperi, 'Otras Indias': missionari della Controriforma tra contadini e selvaggi," in *Scienze, credenze occulte, livelli di cultura* (Florence, 1982), pp. 205–234, especially p. 227; and D. E. Mungello, *Curious Land: Jesuit Accommodation and the Origins of Sinology* (Stuttgart, 1985).

25. *Lettres édifiantes et curieuses*, XIV recueil, introduction, p. xxiv.

26. L. Le Comte, *Nouveaux Mémoires sur l'Etat present de la Chine* (Paris 1697), 1:249. See I. G. Zuparov, "Aristocratic Analogies and Demotic Descriptions in the Seventeenth-Century Madurai Mission," *Representations* 41 (Winter 1993): 123–48, a remarkable case study.

27. *Lettres édifiantes et curieuses*, XIV recueil (Paris, 1720), p. 1ff.

28. *Lettres édifiantes et curieuses*, XIV recueil, pp. 49–50: "Il me répondit froidement: 'Tant pis, mon Père, pour ces barbares, s'ils veulent rester dans leur barbarie; nous tâchons de les rendre hommes, et ils ne le veulent pas, tant pis pour eux, il y a des inconvenients par tout.' Quelques bar bares cependant qu'ils soient, selon certaines maximes du monde Chinois, je les crois plus près de la vraie Philosophie que le grand nombre des plus celebres philosophes de la Chine."

29. See. W. Kaegi, "Voltaire e la disgregazione della concezione cristiana della storia," *Meditazioni storiche*, ed. and trans. D. Cantimori (Bari, 1960), pp. 216–38, especially p. 233.

30. See my paper "Montaigne, Cannibals and Grottoes," *History and Anthropology* 6 (1993): 125–55.

31. *Lettres édifiantes et curieuses*, I recueil, pp. 112ff. (a letter sent from Manila in 1697 to Thyrse Gonzales, general of the Jesuit Order).

32. Cf. R. Syme, *Tacitus* (Oxford, 1958), 2:529, n. 1. See also P. Perrochat in *Revue des Etudes Latines* 13 (1935): 261–65; Schönfeld, *De Taciti studiis Sallustianis* (diss.) (Leipzig, 1884), especially pp. 52–54. Calgacus's harangue inspired Antonio de Guevara's indictment of Roman imperialism, which he put in the mouth of a "Danubian peasant" speaking before the emperor Marcus Aurelius: see A. De Guevara, *El Villano del Danubio y otros fragmentos*, with an introductory essay by A. Castro, Princeton Texts in Literature and the History of Thought, Romance Section, no. 5 (Princeton, 1945). I am grateful to John Elliott, who pointed out the relevance of Guevara's text to me. Le Gobien may have had access to a French translation or adaptation (A. de Guevara, *L'horloge des princes avec le tres renommé livre de Marc Aurele* [Antwerp, 1592], pp. 413–31), which includes many additions emphasizing the theme of Germanic identity.

33. See *C. Cornelii Taciti Opera quae extant Justus Lipsius postremum recensuit . . .* , (Antwerp, 1607), pp. 461–62.

34. Tacitus, *Agricola*, ch. 30 (*Dialogus, Agricola, Germania*, trans. M. Hutton, The Loeb Classical Library [Cambridge, Mass., and London, 1958], pp. 218–19). Calgacus's speech was mentioned by S. Weil in her *Quelques réflexions sur les origines de l'hitlérisme* (written in 1939): see P. Desideri, *Storia di Roma*, ed. A. Schiavone (Turin, 1991), vol. 2, tome 2:595–98.

35. Besides a succinct remark in P. Villey's posthumous work, *Montaigne devant la postérité* (Paris, 1935), pp. 266–67, see F. de Dainville, *L'éducation des Jésuites (XVIe–XVIIIe siècles)*, ed. M.-M. Compère (Paris, 1978), pp. 178, 434. The latter passage is a rephrasing from Dainville's earlier book, *La naissance de l'humanisme moderne* (Geneva, 1969 [1940]), p. 102.

36. Cf. G. Dulong, *L'abbé de Saint-Réal*; A. Mansau, *Saint-Réal et l'humanisme cosmopolite* (Lille, 1976).

37. *Méthode pour étudier l'histoire, qui contient le Traité de l'Usage de l'Histoire, par M. l'abbé de Saint-Réal, un discours sur les Historiens Français par M. de Saint-Evremont, Intructions pour l'histoire, par le P. Rapin de la Compagnie de Jésus, avec un Catalogue des principaux historiens et des Remarques critiques sur la bonté de leurs ouvrages et sur le choix des meilleures Éditions*, ed. Lenglet du Fresnoy (vol. 2, Brussels, 1714). All subsequent quotations from Saint-Réal works are from his *Oeuvres meslées* (Utrecht, 1693).

38. C. Borghero, in his otherwise remarkable book, dismisses Saint-Réal's *De l'usage de l'histoire* as a "rhetorical dissertation" and Bayle's judgment as "an excess of *politesse*" (*La certezza e la storia: Cartesianesimo, pirronismo e conoscenza storica* [Milan, 1983], pp. 297–98).

39. Cf. Saint-Réal, *Oeuvres*, p. 64: "car toutes les idées naturelles doivent être universelles dans tous les temps et dans tous les lieux, et ne souffrent point d'exception."

40. Cf. Saint-Réal, *Oeuvres*, pp. 64–65: "C'est ainsi que raisonnent les esprits forts, et ils triomphent de raporter à ce propos tout ce qu'il y a de plus étrange dans les moeurs et les usages du Nouveau Monde, du Perou, et de la Chine, pour faire voir que l'Opinion est la seule règle des hommes, et que la Nature n'est rien: comme si la raison naissante de ces peuples demi bêtes étoit comparable à la nôtre, consommée par une si longue possession de politesse et de science, et par la connaissance de tout ce qu'il y a jamais eu de civilisé sur la terre."

41. Saint-Réal's passage on Louis XI echoed an argument made by Estienne Pasquier in his *Les recherches de la France*, and strongly denounced by the Jesuit François Garasse, *Les recherches des recherches et autres oeuvres de Me Estienne Pasquier pour la defense de nos Roys, contre les outrages, calomnies, et autres impertinences dudit autheur* (Paris 1622), pp. 85–86.

42. "L'historien sous un masque emprunté, tantôt remontera jusqu'aux premiers principes du droit naturel, et fera connaître à quelles conditions la nature permet aux sociétés d'être heureuses . . .," Bonnot de Mably, "L'historien, le romancier, le poète," p. 7.

43. Le Gobien, *L'Histoire de l'édit de l'Empereur de la Chine*, p. 104, footnote to a letter sent by the Jesuits to the Chinese Emperor: "La Chine a conservé plus de deux mille ans la connoissance du vray Dieu, et elle n'est devenuë idolatre que cinq ou six cents ans avant la naissance de Jesus-Christ."

44. *Censure de la sacrée faculté de Théologie de Paris portée contre*

les propositions extraites des livres intitulés Nouveaux Mémoires sur l'Etat présent de la Chine, Histoire de l'Édit de l'Empereur de la Chine, Lettre des cérémonies de la Chine, n.d.; Le Comte, *Nouveaux Mémoires,* 2:109 (this sentence is quoted, in a condensed form, by Voltaire, *Essai sur les moeurs,* ed. R. Pomeau [Paris, 1963], 1:220).

45. See Le Comte, *Nouveaux Mémoires,* 2:109; see also the "avertissement" to the first volume. On this issue, see D. P. Walker, *The Ancient Theology* (London, 1972), pp. 194–230 ("The Survival of Ancient Theology in Late Seventeenth-Century France and French Jesuit Missionaries in China").

46. The "paradoxes" of the Society of Jesus are emphasized, from an insider's point of view, by O'Malley in his *The First Jesuits,* pp. 21–22 (which I read after having written these pages).

47. Cf. Le Gobien, *Histoire des Isles Marianes,* p. 142, note: "On a peine à croire que ces Insulaires ne fussent sujets aux rheumes et aux fluxions, et qu'ils n'eussent pas d'insectes dans leurs Isles avant l'arrivée des Espagnols. Mais il est certain que ces Barbares leur en ont fait un crime, et qu'ils le leur ont souvent reproché." Both Le Gobien's footnote and the related passage in his text have been tacitly skipped over (probably as irrelevant) in G. Chinard's quotation of Hurao's harangue (Diderot, *Supplément,* p. 119, n. 2).

48. I used a similar approach to misunderstandings within the same text in *The Night Battles* (London and Baltimore, 1983); for further remarks, see my "The Inquisitor as Anthropologist," in *Clues, Myths, and the Historical Method* (Baltimore, 1989), pp. 156–64, as well as, in a context close to the one I am dealing with here, "On the European (Re)discovery of Shamans," *Elementa* 1 (1993): 26–27. In a previous passage (*Histoire des Isles Marianes,* p. 47), Le Gobien had written: "et sur tout la vie libre et unie qu'ils menent sans soin, sans dépendance, sans chagrin, et sans inquiétude, leur donnent une santé qu'on n'a jamais connue en Europe, quelque soin qu'on a apporté, pour se la procurer."

49. See Le Gobien, *Histoire des Isles Marianes,* dedication: "C'est sur les mémoires de ces hommes apostoliques, dont la plupart ont eu le bonheur de donner leur vie pour Jésus-Christ, que j'ai écrit l'histoire que je donne au public." I consulted the Italian translation of García's work (F. Garzia, *Istoria della conversione . . .,* [Naples, 1686]) and a typewritten edition of *Cartas annuas de la provincia de Filipinas de la Compañía de Jesús, 1665–1671—Marianas,* Spanish Typescript by Sr. Felicia E. Plaza, M. M. B., (Agaña, Guam, 1975) (MARC Working Papers, no. 14, Micronesian Area Research Center, University of Guam, 1979). The original ms. is preserved in the Archivo de la Compañía de Jesús de Toledo, Legajo 324, 65 folios, pp. 523–608; there is a copy in the Micronesian Area Research Center, Spanish Documents Collection.

50. *Cartas annuas de la provincia de Filipinas,* p. 56.

51. *Cartas annuas de la provincia de Filipinas,* p. 13: "Persuadíanse que los ratones, moscas, mosquitos y todas sus enfermedades se las habían traído los navíos que pasaban por las islas, dando la prueba desto en los ca-

tarros con que suelen quedar todos los años después de pasados los navíos; y es así que como la codicia del hierro les hace estar voceando alrededor de las naos de día y de noche al sol, al sereno y demás inclemencias de la mar, es forzosa vuelvan los mas roncos y con otros males á sus casas." Another letter (p. 6) mentions "la plaga de ratones y otras lagartijas y animalillos bien enfadosos" in the islands. Those complaints were not exceptional. In a letter written in 1640 Marie Guyart de l'Incarnation mentioned a harangue delivered in an assembly by an elderly Huron woman with authority, who accused the Jesuits of spreading disease through spells, prayers, and a "big pieces of wood" (rifles, Marie de l'Incarnation explained to her correspondent). Evidently, accusations of the kind accompanied in different countries the encounters (often fraught with lethal consequences) between European missionaries and indigenous populations. But the analogy with Hurao's speech reported by Le Gobien was also based on the presence, in both cases, of Jesuit mediation: in the case of Marie de l'Incarnation, the cleric in question was Father Pierre Pijart, who had been present at the Huron woman's harangue (cf. N. Z. Davis, *Women on the Margins: Three Seventeenth-Century Lives* [Cambridge, Mass., 1995], pp. 111–12, 284, n. 180). Hurao's harangue was reprinted in C. des Brosses, *Histoire des navigations aux terre australes*, II (Paris, 1756), pp. 497–98. It was preceded by the following remark: "elle sera certainement du goût d'un célèbre philosophe cynique de notre siècle"—an allusion to Rousseau's *Discours sur les origines de l'inégalité* (1755).

52. See A. W. Crosby, Jr., *The Columbian Exchange: Biological and Cultural Consequences of 1492* (Westport, Conn., 1972), p. 97 (on the diffusion of the Old World black rat).

4   Reflections on a Blank

I

The blank referred to here, arguably the most famous in the history of the novel, occurs toward the end of Flaubert's *L'Éducation sentimentale*, between the fifth and sixth chapters of the third, and last, part of the book. The relevance of the passage was stressed for the first time, if I am not mistaken, by Marcel Proust, in his splendid article on the style of Flaubert, published in *La Nouvelle Revue Française* in 1920.[1]

"In my view," Proust wrote,

the most beautiful thing in *L'Éducation sentimentale* is not a sentence, but a blank. Flaubert has described page after page, in great detail, Frédéric Moreau's actions, including the most irrelevant. Frédéric sees a soldier attacking a rioter with his sword, who falls dead. 'And Frédéric, open-mouthed, recognized Sénécal.' Here we have a blank, an enormous blank, and without transition time flows not by quarters of hours, but by years, by decades (I quote again the last words I mentioned before in order to show the extraordinary, unprepared, change of speed):

"And Frédéric, open-mouthed, recognized Sénécal.

He travelled. He came to know the melancholy of the steamboat, the cold awakening in the tent, etc. He returned.

He went into society, etc.

Toward the end of 1867, etc."

Undoubtedly, in Balzac's novels we often have expressions such as: 'In 1817, the Sécards were, etc.' But in Balzac these shifts in time have either an active or a documentary character. Flaubert is the first to unravel them from parasitical anecdotes and the dregs of history. He is the first to put them into music.[2]

The opposition Proust establishes between two narrative approaches to time, based respectively on "the dregs of history" and on "music" ("scories de l'histoire" and "musique"), provides the starting point for the following reflections.

II

The power with which Flaubert conveyed the flow of time affected Proust for personal reasons, "in so far as," he wrote, "I find in him the solution to my modest attempts" (*parce que j'y retrouve l'aboutissement des modestes recherches que j'ai faites*). Without being particularly fond of Flaubert (a writer, he said, "que je n'aime pas beaucoup"), Proust had felt truly intoxicated by him—a poison he tried to purge from his system by including a "dreadful" pastiche based on Flaubert's style in his series on *L'Affaire Lemoine*.[3] In fact, the comment on Flaubert's blank throws much light on Proust's style as well.

Albert Thibaudet, the French critic whose article (a curious blend of pedestrian and insightful remarks) had triggered Proust's magnificent response, had already indicated the incomparable "variety of cuts" (*variété de coupe*) mastered by Flaubert.[4] A stunning example of one of them, to be added to Thibaudet's list, occurs between the fifth and sixth chapter of the first part of *L'Éducation sentimentale*.

Madame Moreau has just informed Frédéric, her son, that his inheritance is gone. He will have to become a clerk, she explains, in order to try to "make a good marriage.

"Frédéric was no longer listening. He was gazing unthinkingly [*machinalement*] over the hedge, into the garden opposite.

"A little red-haired girl of about twelve was there all alone. She had made herself a pair of earrings with sorb apples . . ." The child is then described for some seven lines. Madame Moreau tells her son that she is their neighbor's daughter, who has recently been made legitimate by her father.[5] The fifth chapter ends.

The sixth chapter begins as follows: "Ruined, robbed, done for!" (*Ruiné, dépouillé, perdu!*). The description of the little girl, seen through the absentminded eyes of Frédéric, postpones his reactions and therefore slows down the narrative. Retrospectively, the reader will realize that the girl's sudden apparition had a nearly prophetic significance, since her father later attempts to marry her to Frédéric—a marriage that would have fulfilled Madame

Moreau's plans. But the first reaction of Flaubert's reader, confronted with the sudden slowing down of the narrative, would have been one of frustration, since it contradicted (as Peter Brooks has convincingly argued) a set of expectations based on Balzac's novels.[6]

On the one hand, a sudden acceleration produced by a blank; on the other, a sudden slowing down produced by an unexpected digression, reinforced by the abrupt ending of the chapter before the emotional climax ("Ruined, robbed, done for!"). The "music" cherished by Proust in Flaubert's novel was a visual music. No pause introduced by one reading the text aloud could provide the shock conveyed by the abrupt shift from one paragraph to the next.[7] A sudden transition within the same paragraph—a device also used by Flaubert—can convey a comparable visual shock. A telling example is the famous passage from *Madame Bovary* in which Emma's romantic dreams suddenly fade into the dull reality of everyday life: "the days, all magnificent, resembled each other like waves; and it [*cela*] swayed on the horizon, infinite, harmonized, azure, and bathed in sunshine. But the child began to cough in her cot or Bovary snored more loudly, and Emma did not fall asleep till morning, when the dawn whitened the window, and when little Justin was already in the square taking down the shutters of the chemist's shop."[8] By using the same verb tense (*cela se balançait . . . Mais l'enfant se mettait à tousser*) Flaubert, as Thibaudet noticed, made Emma's dreams as real as the noises in her room. In commenting on the same passage, Gérard Genette remarked that in the Rouen manuscript of *Madame Bovary* one reads instead "Mais l'enfant tout à coup se mettait à tousser" (But the child suddenly began to cough). By suppressing the temporal adverb *tout à coup* Flaubert enhanced the unexpected continuity between dream and reality.[9]

By inspecting the relevant section in the manuscripts of *L'Éducation sentimentale*, I discovered, with some emotion, the same logic at work. On page after page Flaubert set down, crossed out, and then tirelessly copied again ("Bouvard et Pécuchet, c'est moi!" he could have said) the beginning of the sixth chapter of the third part. In this early manuscript the passage reads "Puis il voyagea" (then he travelled).[10] The temporal adverb was suppressed before publication, according to a consistent pattern aiming, as it has been aptly remarked, at "effects of disjunction."[11] Through that excision the transition became sharper, more abrupt, more consistent with the somber harmony of Flaubert's style: "Il voyagea."

III

[handwritten: Sense of music / Sense of hy]

In this example (one among a thousand) of Flaubert's exacting craftsmanship, Marcel Proust would have presumably seen another victory of "music" over "the dregs of history," *les scories de l'histoire.* My own conclusion is different, and even opposite. It can be shown, using Flaubert as a very special case study, that style and history, far from being mutually exclusive, are in fact related by a mutual interaction.

Proust presented Flaubert's blank as a formal device. It should be pointed out, however, that the blank reinforced a shock generated by a sudden, unexpected twist in the plot of the novel. The manuscript of *L'Éducation sentimentale* shows how this twist came to force itself (so to speak) upon Flaubert. He had first scribbled: "Un murmure d'horreur dans la foule. L'agent la regarde et le cercle s'élargit. Il se remit en marche et Fr[édéric] . . . crut reconn[aître] Sén[écal]." (A whisper of horror in the crowd. The policeman looks around and the circle widens. He walked off and Frédéric believed he had recognized Sénécal.) In the next version he wrote: "Un murmure d'horreur s'éleva de la foule. L'agent en élargit le cercle avec son regard [se remit en marche] et Frédéric . . . [crut reconnaître: crossed out] reconnut [le profil de: crossed out] Sénécal." (A whisper of horror rose from the crowd. The policeman widened the circle with his gaze [walked off] and Frédéric [believed he had recognized] recognized [the profile of] Sénécal.) Then Sénécal's full face appears, and Flaubert finds at last *le mot juste,* the missing adjective he was looking for: "et Frédéric, béant, reconnut Sénécal" (and Frédéric, open-mouthed, recognized Sénécal).[12]

Frédéric's horrified astonishment in recognizing Sénécal as the policeman who had just killed Dussardier is shared by all readers of *L'Éducation sentimentale.*[13] The two characters knew each other, were politically close and—being otherwise as different as possible—moved in the same circles. Dussardier, a shop assistant, a generous Hercules, "whose hair protruded like a bundle of tow from under an oil-cloth cap," is first seen in the act of throwing to the ground a policeman who had brutally kicked a defiant boy during a political demonstration.[14] Sénécal, a teacher of mathematics, is first described through the eyes of Frédéric's friend, Deslauriers, as "a strong-minded fellow with Republican convictions, a future Saint-Just."[15] But when Frédéric meets him, he "did not like the fellow. His hair was cut short like a brush, giving added height to his forehead. There was a cold, hard look in his eyes; and his long black frock-coat, his whole costume, smacked of the pedagogue and the priest."[16] These physiognomical clues turn out to be consistent with Sénécal's convictions:

Every evening, when his work was over, he went home to his attic and searched in his books for a justification of his dreams. He had made notes on the *Contrat social*. He wolfed down the *Revue indépendante*. He was familiar with Mably, Morelly, Fourier, Saint-Simon, Comte, Cabet, Louis Blanc, the whole cartload of Socialist writers—those who wanted to reduce mankind to the level of the barrackroom, send it to the brothel for its amusement, and tie it to the counter or the bench; and out of this mixture he had evolved an ideal of a virtuous democracy, half farm and half factory, a sort of American Sparta in which the individual would exist only to serve Society, which would be more omnipotent, more absolute, more infallible, and more divine than any Gran Lama or Nebuchadnezzar. He had no doubt that this idea would soon be realized, and anything that he considered hostile to it he attacked with the logic of a mathematician and the good faith of an inquisitor. Titles, decorations, plumes, liveries in particular, and even an excessive degree of fame shocked him; and every day his studies and his sufferings added fuel to his hatred of any sort of distinction or superiority.[17]

Flaubert was probably the first writer to exploit fully the potential of free indirect speech (*discours indirect libre*).[18] He used it as a device for distancing himself—without relying on quotation marks—from his characters' words or thoughts, in the very act of presenting them. But in the page quoted above, there is no distance. "Those who wanted to reduce mankind to the level of the barrackroom, send it to the brothel for its amusement, and tie it to the counter or the bench": this is not Sénécal's voice, this is Flaubert's, speaking in fear and horror.[19]

A few days after Louis Napoléon's *coup d'État*, Flaubert had written to his friend Henriette Collier: "Nous allons en France entrer dans une bien triste époque. Et moi je deviens comme l'époque" (In France, we are entering a very sad epoch. And I am becoming like that epoch).[20] The emergence of that unprecedented phenomenon—an Empire receiving its legitimacy from universal suffrage—convinced Flaubert (along with other perceptive conservatives, such as Tocqueville and Burckhardt) that modern societies were heading toward authoritarian democracy of some sort.[21] The trajectory of Sénécal's life unfolds this contradiction. When he is imprisoned before 1848 as a conspirator, his naive comrade, Dussardier, deplores his lot as a victim of Power. On December 2, 1851, Dussardier is killed by Sénécal, the revolutionary turned policeman—a grim anticipation of the twentieth century.[22]

IV

But a formal device such as the blank has a twentieth-century ring as well. Gérard Genette, having remarked that both cinema and Flaubert's style share a resistance to "intériorisation," refers to two details taken from, respectively, *L'Éducation* and *Madame Bovary*, as "gros plans," close-ups.[23] Another critic, Pierre-Marc de Biasi, speaks of Flaubert's habit of fragmenting reality into discrete scenes as an anticipation of cinema.[24] Following these suggestions one is tempted to regard the killing of Dussardier, here quoted in its entirety, as an example of montage *avant la lettre*:

It was five o' clock, and a thin drizzle was falling. The pavement alongside the Opéra was filled with prosperous-looking people. The houses opposite were closed. There was nobody at the windows. Taking up the whole width of the boulevard, some dragoons rode by at full tilt, bent over their horses, with their swords drawn, and the plumes of their helmets, and their great white capes spread out behind them, silhouetted against the light of the gas-lamps, which swung to and fro in the wind and mist. The crowd watched them in terrified silence.

Between the cavalry charges squads of policemen came up to drive the crowds back into the side streets.

But on the steps of Tortoni's a man stood firm, as motionless as a caryatid, and conspicuous from afar on account of his tall stature. It was Dussardier.

One of the policemen, who was marching in front of his squad, with his three-cornered hat pulled down over his eyes, threatened him with his sword.

Then Dussardier took a step forward and started shouting:

"Long live the Republic!"

He fell on his back, with his arms spread out.

A cry of horror rose from the crowd. The policeman looked all around him, and Frédéric, open-mouthed, recognized Sénécal.

VI

He travelled.

He came to know the melancholy of the steamboat, the cold awakening in the tent, the tedium of landscapes and ruins, the bitterness of interrupted friendships.[25]

In a well-known essay, the film director Sergei Eisenstein read Leonardo da Vinci's notes on the representation of the Flood in painting as an example of a "shooting-script."[26] In the case of Flaubert the same experiment would prove to be as effective, although less anachronistic. But the analogy between cinema and some features of Flaubert's style needs clarification. One of the earliest reviewers of *L'Éducation sentimentale*, the critic Édmond Scherer, objected to the novel's exceeding fragmentation by comparing it to a "collection of photographs."[27] A few months earlier Scherer had dismissed Baudelaire as a corrupt writer and "a man devoid of genius."[28] His criticism of *L'Éducation sentimentale*, which elicited Flaubert's sarcastic reaction, was less philistine.[29] In remarking that its episodes "lead nowhere" Scherer anticipated, in a sense, the famous definition of *L'Éducation* provided ten years later by Thédore de Banville: "le roman *non romancé*, triste, indécis, mysterieux comme la vie elle-même" (the unromanced novel, sad, uncertain, mysterious as life itself).[30] But in Scherer's eyes this "indecisiveness" was a major weakness: "A force d'être réaliste," he wrote, "il [Flaubert] est réel, sans doute; mais à force d'être réel, il cesse de nous intéresser" (The more Flaubert becomes a realist, the more he becomes real; but by becoming real, he ceases to interest us). In order to make reality interesting one has to inject meaning into it—which is what photography and Flaubert were, according to Scherer, respectively unable and unwilling to do.[31]

Scherer's reference to photography may have implied an allusion to Maxime Du Camp, one of Flaubert's oldest friends (in their youth they had written a travel diary together, partially published as *Par les champs et par les grèves*). Besides being a writer, Du Camp was a professional photographer. In 1851 he had published a selection of the calotypes he had made while touring for three years with Flaubert in the Orient: three large volumes entitled *Egypte Nubie Syrie: Paysages et Monuments*.[32] The passage in which Flaubert describes Frédéric's travels—"He came to know the melancholy of the steamboat, the cold awakening in the tent, the tedium of landscapes and ruins, the bitterness of interrupted friendships"—sounds like a reference to his own travels with Maxime Du Camp, who echoed the same passage in his *Souvenirs de l'année 1848*: "Je connus la fatigue des lentes patrouilles faites à travers la ville, la mélancolie des nuits passées au poste, l'ennui énervant des longues factions" (I knew the fatigue of the slow marches across the city, the melancholy of the nights spent on guard, the tiring boredom of the long watches).[33] This allusion was appropriate to a memoir in which the names of the three friends— Du Camp himself, Flaubert, and Louis Bouilhet—were repeatedly listed together as witnesses to the events of the 1848 revolution, events reworked in *L'Éducation sentimentale*.[34] In the introduction to his recollections, Du Camp wrote:

Je me décidai à écrire ce que je me rappelais des journées de 22, 23 et 24 février 1848. Mais à mesure que je m'interrogeais, la bobine de ma mémoire s'est dévidée toute seule, comme le tableau mouvant des optiques; j'ai vu repasser devant mes yeux les événements auxquels j'avais assisté.

(I decided to recollect what I remembered of those days—February 22, 23, and 24, 1848. But as I was interrogating myself, the spool of my memory emptied itself, as if it were one of those opticians' moving panels; I saw the events I had witnessed taking place again in front of my eyes.)[35]

"La bobine de ma mémoire s'est dévidée toute seule": for a late-twentieth-century reader this metaphor points inevitably to cinema. The past is a movie, our memory is a projector: "J'ai vu repasser devant mes yeux les événements auxquels j'avais assisté" (I saw passing again before my eyes the events I had once witnessed). But in 1876 the reference must have been different. On a literal level, the "bobine" was the spool of the spinning-jenny, hailed by Maxime Du Camp as one of the symbols of progress in a section of his *Chants modernes*—a book that could have been written by Monsieur Homais, the anticlerical pharmacist of *Madame Bovary*. The "bobine" was listed along with "la vapeur," "la photographie," "la locomotive," and so forth, in a series of poems labelled "Chants de la matière," songs about matter, dedicated to Charles Lambert, a follower of Saint-Simon, who had spent many years in Egypt as director of the École Polytechnique created by Mehemet-Ali.[36] Through the "bobine," the old metaphor of the thread of memory was connected to another piece of modern technology, "le tableau mouvant des optiques"—presumably an allusion to the diorama invented by Daguerre, a decisive link in the historical chain that led to the invention of the cinema.[37] In the section on panoramas in his *Passagen-Werk*, Walter Benjamin remarked that by changing the lights behind the depiction of a sunrise, the diorama had been able to compress into a few minutes a sequence that in nature could last for an hour.[38] This unprecedented experience of acceleration provides the historical context for some of the boldest features of Flaubert's style. When Daguerre proudly speaks of his "décompositions de formes, au moyen desquelles, dans la Messe de Minuit par exemple, des figures apparaissaient où l'on venait de voir des chaises" (decomposing forms, which, like those in the Midnight Mass, make figures appear in the place of chairs),[39] one thinks of another example of "dissolution," the aforementioned transition from the dreams of Emma Bovary to the dull reality around her.

But the new form of vision provided by the diorama was reinforced by the railroad, another of the devices that, according to Du Camp (who dedicates a poem to it) enhanced the senses, transforming humans into gods.[40] As Wolfgang Schivelbusch has brilliantly shown, the railroad presented the astonished traveler (as a contemporary French observer put it) "with happy scenes, sad scenes, burlesque interludes, brilliant fireworks."[41] Flaubert's fragmented style, and in particular his descriptions of urban or country landscapes seen through the eyes of his characters, unfolded the implications of the new technologies, and especially the thrilling experiences provided by the railroad. In the passages that follow Frédéric Moreau is seen, respectively, travelling by train, taking a carriage with Madame Dambreuse, and hopelessly waiting for Madame Arnoux in the streets of Paris crowded with rioters and soldiers:

Green fields stretched away to right and left; the train rolled along; the little station houses glided by like stage sets; and the big, fleecy puffs of smoke from the engine, always falling to the same side, danced on the grass for a moment, then melted away.[42]

She brought him back in her carriage; the rain lashed the windows; the passers-by flitted through the mud like shadows; and, pressed close together, they observed all this dimly, with a calm disdain.[43]

At the far end of the vista, on the boulevard, vague masses of people were moving about. Now and then he made out the plume of a dragoon's helmet, a woman's hat; and he strained his eyes in an attempt to recognize her.[44]

We started with a blank, the striking blank selected by Proust; but the entire prose of Flaubert is fragmented by invisible blanks.[45]

V

Some years ago Maurice Agulhon stressed the importance of *L'Éducation sentimentale* for the historian: as a document, of course, but also as a contribution to our understanding of French society before and after 1848. He focused particularly on *Il voyagea*. Those "astonishingly elliptical words," he wrote, provide Flaubert's "most vigorous historical teaching," since they effectively convey the emptiness felt by a large part of French society when the dictatorship of Louis Napoléon replaced the Republic.[46] In the prevailing intellectual atmosphere, Agulhon's authoritative remark runs the risk of being mistaken as an argument for blurring the distinction between fiction and history. My attitude (as well as, I suppose, Agulhon's) is totally different. I find the current approach to historical narratives highly simplistic, since it usually focuses on the final literary product, disregarding the research (archival, philological, statistical, and so forth) that made it possible.[47] Our attention should shift instead from the end result to the preparatory stages, in order to explore the mutual interaction between empirical data and narrative constraints *within the process of research itself*. Many years ago Lucien Febvre remarked that historical evidence speaks only if properly addressed. This seems quite obvious today. What is less apparent is that the historian's questions are always, either directly or indirectly, in narrative forms (emphasizing the plural). Those provisional narratives provide a set of possibilities, which are often modified, and sometimes rejected, during the process of research. We can compare those narratives to mediating instances between questions and evidence, instances that deeply (although not exclusively) affect the way in which historical data are collected, discarded, interpreted—and then, of course, written. Let us look at just one example, taken from the work of Marc Bloch, the great historian who cofounded and directed, with Lucien Febvre, the journal *Annales d'histoire économique et sociale*. One of Bloch's most original books, *Les caractères originaux de l'histoire rurale française*, is introduced by a few pages, entitled "Quelques observations de méthode," which explain why scholars working on rural societies must, as often as possible, "read history backwards" (*lire l'histoire à rebours*).[48] But this "regressive method," as Bloch calls it, must be employed prudently: "If we use our common sense, we shall see that the picture presented by the recent past is not an image we merely need to project over and over again in order to reproduce that of centuries more and more remote; what the recent past offers resembles rather the last reel of a film which we must try to unroll, resigned to the gaps we shall certainly discover, resolved to pay due regard to its sensitivity as a register of change."[49] Bloch had used the same metaphor in his memoirs of the war, published after his death, and precisely in his recollections of September 10, 1914—the day of his *baptême du feu*, which coincided with the Battle of the Marne. Today we may take for granted the idea of turning the past backwards as with a film reel; it was certainly far less obvious in 1914.[50] The possibility that Bloch's metaphor was a reworking of the image used by Maxime Du Camp in introducing his *Souvenirs de l'année 1848*—"La bobine de ma mémoire s'est dévidée toute seule"—does not seem farfetched. Two months before, in July 1914, in a (also posthumously published) talk on "Critique historique et critique du témoignage" at the Lycée of Amiens, Bloch had mentioned the scholarly debate concerning the *fusillade* that had ignited the 1848 revolution in Paris: who shot first, a soldier or a participant in the rally?[51] It happens that Maxime Du Camp's main purpose, in publishing his recollections of 1848 thirty years after, had been precisely to clarify the famous episode on the basis of his own testimony, which (according to such an expert as Maurice Agulhon) finally settled the debate.[52] Given Bloch's interest in the shooting of February 23, 1848, a familiarity with Maxime Du Camp's *Souvenirs* is more than likely. But in his last reflections on method, posthumously published as *Métier d'historien* (The historian's craft) Bloch quoted the passage on the *fusillade* from his youthful essay, adding a significant remark: even the impossibility of arriving at a conclusion about this sort of event would not affect history in its most profound and genuine dimension.[53] *Les caractères originaux de l'histoire rurale française* is an example of what Bloch meant by "histoire plus profonde et plus vraie." Was Bloch, in writing his history backwards, inspired by his passion for the cinema? Was he, in accepting gaps or *trous* in the evidence as part of his narrative, inspired by Flaubert? We will probably never know. But the very availability of a narrative device can generate—either directly or indirectly, by raising a silent veto—a specific approach to research.[54]

All this is a far cry from the ornamental notion of rhetoric suggested by Cicero—*rem tene, et verba sequentur* (get the argument and words will follow)—a notion inadvertently shared by those late-twentieth-century skeptics who insist on separating historical narratives from the research on which they are based. The essay by Marcel Proust with which this chapter began suggests a more profound approach. In reacting to Albert Thibaudet's dismissive tone, Proust wrote:

> I was astonished, I must confess, to see that one could consider to be a scarcely gifted writer a man who, through his use of the past tense, of the imperfect tense, of the present participle, of certain pronouns and certain prepositions, has renovated our vision of things nearly as deeply as Kant, with his Categories and his theories about Knowledge and the reality of the external world.[55]

These are strong, emphatic words. But I think that Proust was absolutely correct in stressing, not only the cognitive richness of Flaubert's work, but also the cognitive potential of narratives in general. As this chapter intended to show, they play an important role not only in so-called narrative history (a somewhat awkward notion) but in every form of historical research and writing, including the most analytical.

Notes

1. M. Proust, "A propos du 'style' de Flaubert," *Chroniques* (Paris, 1927), pp. 193–211 (first published in *Nouvelle Revue français*, January 1920). The long-term impact of this essay is attested to, for instance, by A. Cento, *Il realismo documentario nell'*Éducation sentimentale' (Naples, 1967).

2. M. Proust, *Chroniques*, pp. 205–206:
A mon avis la chose la plus belle de l'*Education Sentimentale*, ce n'est pas une phrase, mais un blanc. Flaubert vient de décrire, de rapporter pendant de longues pages, les actions les plus menues de Frédéric Moreau. Frédéric voit un agent marcher avec son épée sur un insurgé qui tombe mort. "Et Frédéric, béant, reconnut Sénécal." Ici un "blanc," un énorme "blanc" et, sans l'ombre d'une transition, soudain la mesure du temps devenant au lieu de quarts d'heure, des années, des décades (je reprends les dernier mots que j'ai cités pour montrer cet extraordinaire changement de vitesse, sans préparation):
"Et Frédéric, béant, reconnut Sénécal.

Il voyagea. Il connut la mélancolie des paquebots, les froids réveils sous la tente, etc. Il revint.

Il fréquenta le monde, etc.
Vers la fin de l'année 1867, etc."
Sans doute, dans Balzac, nous avons bien souvent: "En 1817 les Séchard étaient, etc." Mais chez lui ces changements de temps ont un caractère actif ou documentaire. Flaubert le premier les débarasse du parasitisme des anecdotes et des scories de l'histoire. Le premier, il les met en musique.

3. M. Proust, *Pastiches et mélanges* (Paris, 1970), pp. 9–22; W. Pabst and L. Schrader, eds., *L'Affaire Lemoine von Marcel Proust: Kommentare und Interpretationen* (Berlin, 1972), especially pp. 40–77 (essays by I. Sorhagen, C. Haselbach, L. Schrader). The pastiche was, Proust said, "détestable d'ailleurs."

4. A. Thibaudet, "Sur le style de Flaubert," *Nouvelle Revue française* 13 (1919): 942–53, especially p. 951: "Dans l'intérieur de ses limites, un peu étroites, cette prose est d'une délicatesse de rythmes, d'une science et d'une variété de coupe incomparables. Avec La Bruyère et Montesquieu, Flaubert paraît dans la langue le maître de la coupe; nul n'a de virgules plus significatives, d'arrêts de tous genres plus nerveux."

5. G. Flaubert, *Sentimental Education*, trans. R. Baldick (Harmondsworth, 1979), p. 99; *L'Éducation sentimentale*, ed. E. Maynial (Paris, 1954), pp. 90–91.

6. P. Brooks, "Retrospective Lust, or Flaubert's Perversities," in *Reading for the Plot* (Cambridge, Mass., 1992), pp. 171–215.

7. The importance of *alinéas* is stressed by Jean Bruneau, the editor of the new critical edition of Flaubert's correspondence, with a reference to the blank we are discussing: see G. Flaubert, *Correspondance* (Paris, 1973), I:xxiv–xxv.

8. G. Flaubert, *Madame Bovary*, trans. M. W. Dunne (New York, 1904), p. 122; (*Madame Bovary*, Paris, 1972), p. 259: "les jours, tous magnifiques, se ressemblaient comme des flots; et cela se balançait à l'horizon, infini, harmonieux, bleuâtre et couvert de soleil. Mais l'enfant se mettait à tousser dans son berceau, ou bien Bovary ronflait plus fort, et Emma ne s'endormait que le matin, quand l'aube blanchissait les carreaux et que déjà le petit Justin, sur la place, ouvrait les auvents de la pharmacie," quoted by G. Genette, "Silences de Flaubert," in *Figures* (Paris, 1966), I:223–43.

9. Genette, "Silences," p. 227. The equally abrupt contiguity of dissonant passages within the same paragraph creates a similar effect, as in Proust's description of the death of Bergotte in front of Vermeer's *View of Delft*: "He repeated to himself: 'Little patch of yellow wall, with a sloping roof, little patch of yellow wall.' While doing so he sank down upon a circular divan; and then at once he ceased to think that his life was in jeopardy and, reverting to his natural optimism, told himself: 'It is just an ordinary indigestion from those potatoes; they weren't properly cooked; it is nothing.' A fresh attack beat him down: he rolled from the divan to the floor, as visitors and attendants came hurrying to his assistance. He was dead. Permanently dead? Who shall say? Certainly our experiments in

spiritualism prove no more than the dogmas of religion that the soul survives death, etc." M. Proust, *Remembrance of Things Past*, trans. C. K. Scott Moncrieff (New York, 1932), *The Captive*, 2:509; *A la recherche du temps perdu*, ed. P. Clarac and A. Ferré (Paris, 1954), *La prisonnière*, 3:187: "Il se répétait: 'Petit pan de mur jaune avec un auvent, petit pan de mur jaune.' Cependant il s'abattit sur un canapé circulaire; aussi brusquement il cessa de penser que sa vie était en jeu et, revenant à l'optimisme, se dit: 'C'est une simple indigestion que m'ont donnée ces pommes de terre pas assez cuites, ce c'est rien.' Un nouveau coup l'abattit, il roula du canapé par terre, où accoururent tous les visiteurs et gardiens. Il était mort. Mort à jamais? Qui peut le dire? Certes, les expériences spirites pas plus que les dogmes religieux n'apportent de preuve que l'âme subsiste [etc.]" The transition from straightforward narrative to metaphysical questioning is so unexpected, and so powerful, because it takes place within the same paragraph.

    10. Paris, Bibliothèque Nationale, *Nouv. acq. fr.* 17610, 63v, 64r, 65r, 71v, 77v. I wish to thank Madame Odile de Guidis, of the Institut des Textes et Manuscrits modernes, who kindly sent me a photocopy of this section of the manuscript.

    11. See P. M. Wetherill, "Le style des thèmes: Étude sur le dernier manuscrit autographe de *L'Éducation sentimentale*," *Zeitschrift für französische Sprache und Literatur*, 81 (1971): 308–51 (instances of suppression of *puis*: pp 341–42) and 82 (1972), 1–51.

    12. Paris, Bibliothèque Nationale, *Nouv. acq. fr.* 17610, 53v, 61r, 62r. Maxime Du Camp, in revising the manuscript of *L'Éducation*, voiced his dissatisfaction: "*Béant* est bien faux à mon avis; c'est une épithète physique pour rendre une impression morale—avec un mot plus simple, épouvanté—stupéfait—indigné, je ne sais quoi, tu feras plus d'effet." Flaubert kept "béant," laconically referring in his notes to Buffon's theory of images: see P. M. Wheterill, "Le dernier stade de la composition de *L'Éducation sentimentale*," *Zeitschrift für französische Sprache und Literatur*, 78 (1968) 229–52, especially 252.

    13. Although readers have been somewhat forewarned by some passages from the previous chapter (ch. 4):

    Sénécal . . . parla de sa personne, et des affaires du pays.

    Si lamentables qu'elles fussent, elles le réjouissaient; car on marchait au communisme. . . . Sénécal se déclara pour l'Autorité . . . Vive la tyrannie, pourvu que le tyran fasse le bien! . . . Les conservateurs parlaient maintenant comme Sénécal. (*L'Éducation sentimentale*, pp. 374, 390; *Sentimental Education*, pp. 369, 385)

    14. Flaubert, *Sentimental Education*, p. 41; *L'Éducation sentimentale*, pp. 44–45.

    15. Flaubert, *Sentimental Education*, p. 36; *L'Éducation sentimentale*, p. 38.

    16. Flaubert, *Sentimental Education*, p. 61; *L'Éducation sentimentale*, p. 51: "Ce garçon déplut à Frédéric. Son front était rehaussé par la coupe de ses cheveux taillés en brosse. Quelque chose de dur et de froid perçait dans

ses yeux gris; et sa longue redingote noire, tout son costume sentait le péd-
agogue et l'ecclésiastique."
    17. Flaubert, *Sentimental Education* (translation somewhat modified),
pp. 141–42; *L'Éducation sentimentale*, pp. 136–37:
    Chaque soir, quand sa besogne était finie, il regagnait sa mansarde, et il
    cherchait dans les livres de quoi justifier ses rêves. Il avait annoté *le
    Contrat social*. Il se bourrait de *la Revue indépendante*. Il connaissait
    Mably, Morelly, Fourier, Saint-Simon, Comte, Cabet, Louis Blanc, la
    lourde charretée des écrivains socialistes, ceux qui réclament pour
    l'humanité le niveau des casernes, ceux qui voudraient la divertir dans
    un lupanar ou la plier sur un comptoir; et, du mélange de tout cela, il
    s'était fait un idéal de démocratie vertueuse, ayant le double aspect
    d'une métairie et d'une filature, une sorte de Lacédémone américaine
    où l'individu n'existerait que pour servir la Société, plus omnipotente,
    absolue, infaillible et divine que les Grand Lamas et les Nabuchodono-
    sors. Il n'avait pas un doute sur l'éventualité prochaine de cette concep-
    tion; et tout ce qu'il jugeait lui être hostile, Sénécal s'acharnait dessus,
    avec des raisonnements de géometre et une bonne foi d'inquisiteur. Les
    titres nobiliaires, les croix, les panaches, les livrées surtout, et même
    les réputations trop sonores le scandalisaient,—ses études comme ses
    souffrances avivant chaque jour sa haine essentielle de toute distinc-
    tion ou supériorité quelconque.
Flaubert's derogatory tone in this passage is stressed, among others, by P.
Collet, "Discours et vision politique dans *l'Éducation sentimentale*," in
Analyses et réflexions sur l'Éducation sentimentale (Paris, 1989), p. 59.
    18. A. Thibaudet, *Gustave Flaubert* (Paris, 1935), pp. 247ff.; R. Pascal,
*The Dual Voice: Free Indirect Speech and Its Functioning in the
Nineteenth-Century European Novel* (Manchester, 1977), pp. 98—112; C.
Prendergast, *The Order of Mimesis: Balzac, Stendhal, Nerval, Flaubert*
(Cambridge, 1986), pp. 185—86 (on quotations without quotation marks).
I owe these references, with the exception of the first, to Franco Moretti.
    19. See Pascal, *The Dual Voice*, p. 100, on a few comparable intrusions
of Flaubert's authorial voice in *Madame Bovary*.
    20. G. Flaubert, *Correspondance* (Paris, 1980), 2:19–20 (8 December
1851).
    21. P.-M. de Biasi (Flaubert, *Carnets de travail*, p. 345) "ce que Flaubert
met . . . en scène c'est, ni plus ni moins, l'alliance objective qui est en train
de se nouer historiquement entre un certain socialisme utopique et les in-
térêts du grand capital." Sénécal would embody this historical ambiguity.
But see, for a broader perspective, V. Brombert, *The Novels of Flaubert*
(Princeton, 1966); *La production du sens chez Flaubert*, ed. C. Gothot-
Mersch, et al. (Paris, 1975).
    22. The passage on Sénécal's political ideas (see above, note 17) is
quoted by B. Souvarine, *Stalin*, Italian trans. G. Bartoli (Milan, 1983), p.
655. In reviewing Souvarine's book (1935), Pierre Kaan spoke of "étatisme
à la Flaubert." See G. Bataille, *Contre-attaques*, ed. M. Galletti (Rome,
1995), p. 138.

23. Genette, *Figures*, pp. 228–30.
24. P.-M. de Biasi, "Flaubert," in *Encyclopaedia Universalis, Corpus* 9 (1990): 525; P.-M. de Biasi in G. Flaubert, *Carnets de travail* (Paris, 1988), p. 427.
25. G. Flaubert, *Sentimental Education*, pp. 411–12; *L'Éducation sentimentale*, pp. 418–19:

Il était cinq heures, une pluie fine tombait. Des bourgeois occupaient le trottoir du côté de l'Opéra. Les maisons d'en face étaient closes. Personne aux fenêtres. Dans toute la largeur du boulevard, des dragons galopaient, à fond de train, penchés sur leurs chevaux, le sabre nu; et les crinières de leurs casques, et leurs grands manteaux blancs soulevés derrière eux passaient sur la lumière des becs de gaz, qui se tordaient au vent dans la brume. La foule les regardait, muette, terrifiée.

Entre les charges de cavalerie, des escouades de sergents de ville survenaient, pour faire refluer le monde dans les rues.

Mais, sur les marches de Tortoni, un homme,—Dussardier,—remarquable de loin à sa haute taille, restait sans plus bouger qu'une cariatide.

Un des agents, qui marchait en tête, le tricorne sur les yeux, le menaça de son épée.

L'autre alors, s'avançant d'un pas, se mit à crier:
—Vive la République!
Il tomba sur le dos, le bras en croix.

Un hurlement d'horreur s'éleva de la foule. L'agent fit un cercle autour de lui avec son regard; et Frédéric, béant, reconnut Sénécal.

VI

Il voyagea.
Il connut la mélancolie des paquebots, les froids réveils sous la tente, l'étourdissement des paysages et des ruines, l'amertume des sympathies interrompues.

26. S. Eisenstein, *Film Form: Essays in Film Theory and the Film Sense*, ed. J. Leyda (Cleveland, 1957), pp. 25ff.
27. É. Scherer, *Études sur la littérature contemporaine* (Paris, 1886), 4:293–303, "Un roman de M. Flaubert" (December 1869), especially pp. 296–97: "L'ouvrage n'est pas composé. Nous voyons passer devant nous des personnages, des scènes, mais comme au hasard. On dirait une suite de médaillons, une collection de photographies . . . Les épisodes ne mènent à rien."
28. Scherer, *Études sur la littérature contemporaine*, 4:281–91, "Baudelaire" (July 1869), especially p. 269.
29. G. Flaubert, *Correspondance*, ed. R. Descharmes (Paris, 1924), 3:232.
30. T. de Banville, *Critiques*, ed. V. Barrucand (Paris, 1917), p. 160: "Le roman *non romancé*, triste, indécis, mysterieux comme la vie elle-même, et se contentant, comme elle, de dénouements d'autant plus terribles qu'ils ne sont pas *matériellement* dramatiques" (quoted by Genette, *Fig-*

ures, p. 241, n. 1, who corrects a misprint, "ville" instead of "vie"; the article was written in 1880, after the death of Flaubert).

31. Scherer, *Études sur la littérature contemporaine*, 4:295: "Or, pour nous intéresser, il faut qu'il [l'art] nous parle, et, pour nous parler, il faut qu'il prête un sens aux choses, ou, ce qui revient au même, qu'il en dégage le sens caché."

32. The copy I consulted (at the UCLA Special Collections Library) bears Du Camp's handwritten dedication and was owned by Pierre Louÿs.

33. Du Camp, *Souvenirs de l'année 1848* (Paris, 1876), p. 130, quoted by D. Oster in his introduction to M. Du Camp, *Souvenirs littéraires* (Paris, 1994), p. 41 (see also p. 18). See also J. Ballerini, "The invisibility of Hadji-Ishmael: Maxime Du Camp's 1850 photographs of Egypt," *The Body Imaged*, ed. K. Adler and M. Pointon (Cambridge, 1993), pp. 147–60; J.-M. Carré, *Voyageurs et écrivains français en Égypte*, 2nd ed. (Cairo, 1956): 2:81–134.

34. Du Camp, *Souvenirs de l'année 1848*, pp. 40, 51, 56, 77, 85.

35. Du Camp, *Souvenirs de l'année 1848*, p. 2.

36. Du Camp, *Les Chants modernes*, nouv. éd. (Paris, 1860), p. 172ff. There is an imposing picture of Charles Lambert (then Charles Lambert-Bey) in Carré, *Voyageurs et écrivains*, vol. 2, 1st ed. (Cairo, 1932), facing p. 96. See also Du Camp, *Souvenirs littéraires*, p. 408ff.; P. Bonnefon, "Maxime Du Camp et les Saint-Simoniens," *Revue d'Histoire littéraire de la France* 17 (1910): 709–35; C. L. de Liefde, *Le Saint-Simonisme dans la poésie française entre 1825 et 1865* (Haarlem, 1927); P.-M. de Biasi, "Le projet flaubertien et l'utopie du vouloir conclure," *Littérature*, no. 22 (May 1976): 47–58. Thibaudet rightly remarks ("Sur le style de Flaubert," p. 947) that "La destinée intelligente avait d'ailleurs placeé M. Homais à coté de lui [Flaubert] sous le nom de Maxime du Camp."

37. J. J. Hittorff, "Origine des panoramas," *Revue générale de l'architecture* 2 (1841): 227; G. Bapst, *Essai sur l'histoire des panoramas et des dioramas* (Paris, 1891), p. 20: "Les dioramas étaient fixes, et la salle des spectateurs mobile. Elle portait sur un pivot à son centre, et était maintenue, à son pourtour, par des galets sur lesquels elle glissait en tournant sur elle-même, au moyen d'un manège établi dans les fondations. Un seul homme pouvait la mettre en mouvement." See also H. and A. Gernsheim, *L. J. M. Daguerre: The History of the Diorama and the Daguerreotype*, 2nd ed. (New York, 1968), especially pp. 42ff.

38. W. Benjamin, *Das Passagen-Werk* (Frankfurt am Main 1982) (=W. Benjamin, *Parigi capitale del XIX secolo*, ed. R. Tiedemann [Turin, 1986], pp. 679–89, "Panorama," especially p. 168).

39. L. J. M. Daguerre, *Historique et description des procédés du Daguerréotype et du Diorama* (Paris, 1839), pp. 75ff ("Descriptions des procédés de peinture et d'éclairage inventés par Daguerre, et appliqués par lui aux tableaux du Diorama"). See also Bapst, *Essai*, p. 20.

40. Du Camp, *Chants modernes*, p. 185: "À nous le ciel, la terre et l'onde, / À nous la flamme des cerveaux, / À nous la nature profonde, / Car nous sommes les dieux nouveaux! / Nous centuplons les sens de

l'homme, / Et l'Eden lui sera rendu: / Sans péché qu'il morde à la pomme / Qui brille à l'arbre défendu / [etc.]."

41. W. Schivelbusch, *The Railway Journey: The Industrialization of Time and Space in the 19th Century* (Berkeley, 1986), p. 61 (the book was brought to my attention by Paul Holdengräber), quoting B. Gastineau, *La Vie en chemin de fer* (Paris, 1861), p. 31.

42. Flaubert, *Sentimental Education*, p. 194; *L'Éducation sentimentale*, p. 191: "A droite et à gauche, des plaines vertes s'étendaient; le convoi roulait; les maisonnettes des stations glissaient comme des décors, et la fumée de la locomotive versait toujours du même côté des gros flocons qui dansaient sur l'herbe quelque temps, puis se dispersaient."

43. Flaubert, *Sentimental Education*, p. 368; *L'Éducation sentimentale*, p. 373: "Elle le ramenait dans sa voiture; la pluie fouettait les vasistas; les passants, tel que des ombres, s'agitaient dans la boue; et, serrés l'un contre l'autre, ils apercevaient tout cela confusément, avec un dédain tranquille."

44. Flaubert, *Sentimental Education*, p. 278 (modified); *L'Éducation sentimentale*, p. 280: "Au fond de la perspective, sur le boulevard, des masses confuses glissaient. Il distinguait parfois l'aigrette d'un dragon, un chapeau de femme; et il tendait ses prunelles pour la reconnaître."

45. See also, in a different (but convergent) perspective, M. Nadeau's introduction to *Madame Bovary* (Paris, 1972), especially p. 17.

46. M. Agulhon, "Peut-on lire en historien *L'Éducation sentimentale*?," in *Histoire et langage dans 'L'Éducation sentimentale' de Flaubert* (Paris, 1981), pp. 35–41, especially p. 41: "Pour nous faire sentir la coupure que toute une partie de la société française a ressentie lorsque la dictature bonapartiste a remplacé la République, ces quelques mots prodigieusement elliptiques de *L'Éducation sentimentale* valent toutes les trompettes de *Châtiments*."

47. See B. Croce, "La storia ridotta sotto il concetto generale dell'arte" (1895) (republished in *Primi saggi* [Bari, 1927]), followed by H. White, *Metahistory*: see my paper "Just One Witness," in *Probing the Limits of Representation: Nazism and the "Final Solution,"* ed. S. Friedlander (Cambridge, Mass., 1992), pp. 82–96, 350–55.

48. M. Bloch, *French Rural History* (Berkeley, 1966), p. xxviii; *Les caractères originaux de l'histoire rurale française* (1931), (Paris, 1955), p. xii: "L'historien est toujours l'esclave de ses documents; plus que tout autres, ceux qui se vouent aux études agraires; sous peine de ne pouvoir épeler le grimoire du passé, il leur faut, le plus souvent, lire l'histoire à rebours."

49. Bloch, *French Rural History*, p. xxx; *Les caractères originaux*, p. xiv: "Au proche passé la méthode regressive, sainement pratiquée, ne demande pas une photographie qu'il suffirait ensuite de projeter, toujours pareille à elle-même, pour obtenir l'image figée d'âges de plus en plus lointains; ce qu'elle prétend saisir, c'est la dernière pellicule d'un film, qu'elle s'efforcera ensuite de dérouler à reculons, résignée à y découvrir plus d'un trou, mais décidée à en respecter la mobilité."

50. See M. Bloch, *Souvenirs de guerre, 1914–1915* (Paris, 1969), p. 14:

"Il est probable que tant que je vivrai, à moins que je ne finisse mes jours dans l'imbécillité, je n'oublierai jamais le 10 septembre 1914. Mes souvenirs de cette journée ne sont pourtant pas extrêmement précis. Surtout ils s'enchaînent assez mal. Ils forment une série discontinue d'images, à la vérité très vives, mais médiocrement coordonnées, comme un rouleau cinématographique qui présenterait par places des grandes déchirures et dont on pourrait, sans que l'on s'en aperçut, invertir certains tableaux." The passage is quoted by U. Raulff, *Ein Historiker um 20. Jahrhundert: Marc Bloch* (Frankfurt am Main, 1995), pp. 71-72. Bloch was a passionate moviegoer (p. 118).

51. M. Bloch, "Critique historique et critique du témoignage," *Annales: Économies, Sociétés, Civilisations* 5 (1950): 1-8.

52. M. Agulhon, "Maxime du Camp, témoin de la bourgeoisie de 1848," *Histoire vagabonde* (Paris, 1988), 1:232-39, especially p. 235.

53. Bloch, *Mérie d'historien . . .* , ch. 3. See C. Ginzburg, "A proposito della raccolta dei saggi storici di Marc Bloch," *Studi medievali* 3, no. 6 (1965): 335-53; P. Toubert, "Genesi e fortuna di un libro di Marc Bloch: *Les caractères originaux de l'histoire rurale française*," *La Cultura* (1993): 283-394.

54. The following paragraphs are a reworking, from a different perspective, of suggestions I made in two previous papers: "Vetoes and Compatibilities," *The Art Bulletin* 77 (1995): 534-37; "Making Things Strange: The Prehistory of a Literary Device," *Representations* 56 (1996): 8-28. See also E. H. Gombrich, *Art and Illusion* (London, 1962), on the idea that "making comes before matching."

55. M. Proust, *Chroniques* (Paris, 1927), p. 193: "J'ai été stupéfait, je l'avoue, de voir traiter de peu doué pour écrire, un homme qui par l'usage entièrement nouveau et personnel qu'il a fait du passé défini, du passé indéfini, du participe présent, de certains pronoms et de certains prépositions, a renouvelé presque autant notre vision de choses que Kant, avec ses Catégories, les théories de la Connaissance et de la Réalité du monde extérieur." As Paul Holdengräber pointed out to me, Proust's essay "De la lecture" (1905; Arles, 1994, p. 55), includes a footnote that begins: "J'avoue que certain emploi de l'imparfait de l'indicatif—de ce temps cruel qui nous présente la vie comme quelque chose d'éphémère à la fois et de passif . . ."

Index

UNIVERSITY PRESS OF NEW ENGLAND publishes books under its own imprint and is the publisher for Brandeis University Press, Dartmouth College, Middlebury College Press, University of New Hampshire, Tufts University, and Wesleyan University Press.

Library of Congress Cataloging-in-Publication Data
Ginzburg, Carlo.
History, rhetoric, and proof / Carlo Ginzburg.
    p.   cm. — (The Menahem Stern Jerusalem lectures)
Includes index.
ISBN 0–87451–932–2 (hardcover : alk. paper). — ISBN 0-87451-933-0
(pbk. : alk. paper)
        1. Historiography. 2. Aristotle—Contributions in the philosophy of history. 3. Valla, Lorenzo, 1406–1457. De falso credita et ementita Constantini donatione declamatio. 4. Rhetoric. 5. Jesuits. I. Title.
II. Series.
D13.G4 1999
907'.2—dc 21   99–26979

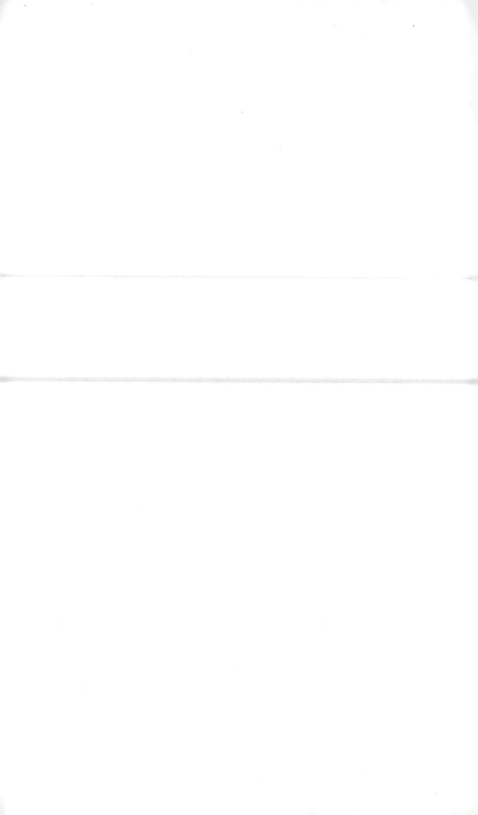